THAT WAY AND THIS

Poetry for Creative Dance

CHOSEN BY
Frances Baldwin
AND
Margaret Whitehead

1972
CHATTO & WINDUS
LONDON

Published by
Chatto & Windus (Educational) Ltd
42 William IV Street
London WC2N 4DF

ISBN 7011 1856 3 (hardback)
ISBN 7011 1857 1 (paperback)

Introduction
selection and notes

© Frances Baldwin and
Margaret Whitehead 1972

Printed in Great Britain by
Redwood Press Limited
Trowbridge, Wiltshire

THAT WAY AND THIS

CONTENTS

5

ACKNOWLEDGEMENTS

The editors and publishers wish to thank the following for permission to reprint copyright material. Every possible effort has been made to trace the copyright owner of each poem included. If any errors or omissions have occured the publishers will be pleased to make correction.

The Literary Trustees of Walter de la Mare and the Society of Authors for 'The Ride by Night', 'The Witch', 'The Snowflake' and 'All the Fun'. James Nimmo Britton for 'Space Travellers'. James Reeves and Oxford University Press for 'Fireworks' from *The Blackbird in the Lilac*. James Reeves and William Heinemann for 'Stocking and Shirt' from *The Wandering Moon*. Carl Sandburg, Holt Rinehart and Winston Inc., and Jonathan Cape for 'Fog' and 'Choose' from *Chicago Poems*, and Carl Sandburg, Harcourt Brace Jovanovich, Inc., for 'Fourth of July Night' from *Wind Song* (copyright 1960 Carl Sandburg). James Kirkup for 'Tea in a Space Ship' and 'Earthquake'. The Executors of the Estate of Robert Bridges and the Clarendon Press, Oxford for 'London Snow'. Frances Horner for 'Fog'. Allen Curnow for 'Wild Iron'. Laurence Pollinger Ltd. and the Estate of the late Mrs. Frieda Lawrence for 'Storm in the Black Forest', 'Bare Almond Trees', 'Bat', 'Humming Bird'. 'Peace', 'Wages', and 'People' from *The Complete Poems of D.H. Lawrence*. The Society of Authors and the literary representative of the Estate of John Masefield for 'Port of Holy Peter' and 'Spanish Waters'. Clarendon Press, Oxford for 'The Sea' by M.J. Josey and 'One Afternoon' by Martin Pepler from *Every Man will Shout* edited by Roger Mansfield and Isobel Armstrong (1964). Celia Mayes for 'The Land'. J. Garnet Miller Ltd. for 'That is Rain on Dry Ground' from *The Boy with a Cart by Christopher Fry*. Mrs. Nicolete Gray and the Society of Authors on behalf of the Laurence Binyon Estate for 'The Builders', and 'Ezekiel'. Faber and Faber for 'The Express' by Stephen Spender from *Collected Poems*. Deborah Bestwick for 'Lines'. Mrs. Bambridge for 'The Secret of the Machines' from *The Definitive Edition of Rudyard Kipling's Verse*. Peter Champkin for 'Jingle for Children' from *Poems of Our Time*. Hubert Nicholson for 'The Man in the Bowler Hat' and 'The British' by A.S.J. Tessimond. E.E. Cummings and MacGibbon and Kee for 'maggie and milly and molly and may' from *Complete Poems 1936-1963* and 'hist whist' from *Complete Poems 1913-1925*. Faber and Faber for 'The Feel of Hands' by Thom Gunn from *My Sad Captains*. G.T. Sassoon for 'Everyone Sang' by Siegfried Sassoon. Faber and Faber for 'Prayer before Birth' from *The Collected Poems of Louis Macneice*. R. Hodgson for 'The Hammers'. William Carlos Williams, New Directions Publishing Corporation and MacGibbon and Kee the 'The Term' from *The Collected Earlier Poems*. Punch for

'The Water Zoo'. Robert Graves for 'Flying Crooked' and 'In Broken Images' from *Collected Poems 1965*. Faber and Faber for 'Chorus VII' from *The Rock, T.S. Eliot*. (Note: see page 122). Rosemary Marriott for 'The Heffalumps'. Galliard Ltd. for 'Lord of the Dance' copyright 1963 from *Songs of Sydney Carter in the Present Tense, Book 2*. Anne Sexton for 'Her Kind' from *Selected Poems*. *Vachel Lindsay* and the Macmillan Company, New York, for 'The Daniel Jazz' and 'The Congo' from *Collected Poems*. The National Christian Education Council for 'Jack Frost' by Cecily E. Pike. Elizabeth Powell for 'The Death Dance of the Whirly Gums'. Frank A. Collymore for 'The Zobo Bird'. George Bell for 'Song from 'Callirrhoe' by Michael Field. A.D. Peters and Co. for 'The End of the Road' from *Sonnets and Verse by Hilaire Belloc*. Faber and Faber for 'Parlour Piece' by Ted Hughes from *Hawk in the Rain*. Faber and Faber for 'The Labyrinth' by Edwin Muir from *Collected Poems 1921-1958*. Charles Causeley and Rupert Hart Davies for 'Healing of a Lunatic Boy' from *Johnny Alleluia*. Faber and Faber for 'The Leaping Laughers' by George Barker from *Collected Poems 1930-1955*.

9

INTRODUCTION

This anthology has been compiled for all those interested in creative movement and who have some basic knowledge of its teaching. The emphasis is on movement work leading to dance and dance drama and a wide range of poems has been selected to enable teachers in primary and secondary schools, students, lecturers and recreational groups to find poetry that will stimulate both movement study and dance composition. None of the poems was written for this purpose and they are first of all to be appreciated in their own right. Teachers and dancers have become so used to the idea of music as the primary partner of dance that many other forms of sound are often neglected. To combine poetry with dance may be a relatively new concept for some and it may therefore be useful to examine the place of this particular partnership within the arts.

Movement and Poetry within the Arts

Art forms are the channels through which we can express ourselves most deeply and communicate with others most fully. Life itself lies constantly open for our interpretation and these are the outlets for convictions we hold, truths we find, and meanings we grasp at. Every element of life may be transposed and brought apart from our purely functional involvement within it through artistic transformation in one medium or another.

Movement has been called the primary art form, and dance the mother of the arts. Music and song grew as accompaniments to dance, and theatre from the masks and costumes that were used. The visual arts sprang from functional and ritual decoration of bodies, clothes and the home.

We neglect a vital element in experiencing and in teaching dance if we ignore concepts shared with other art forms. Only the techniques of becoming familiar with a chosen medium are different in each case, for instance the mastery of the body, the paint, the chisel, the violin. The intrinsic nature

11

of problems, achievements and experiences do not differ.

As well, therefore, as finding out what is involved in enjoying creative movement or how we consciously produce a work of art in dance form, we may look also to other arts most closely allied to movement and discover what is shared with them, where the differences lie, and what may be learned.

Movement takes place in space and has this in common with the visual arts. There are many problems and considerations that are shared, particularly those concerning the arrangement of shape, mass and line in both two dimensions and three. However, a basic difference will affect the approach of the dancer and the painter or sculptor. The two latter may take as much time as they wish or as little — this does not have any bearing on the end result which remains a visual spatial statement. A dancer shares the same use of space, but can never stand apart from the medium, he is physically and instantly a part of it. Movement takes place in time; after the statement has been made it no longer visibly exists. This is an important common factor shared with sound, which also takes place in time and is bound by it. Despite the filming of movement and recording of sound, both acts are initially 'live' and as such will never be identically repeated again.

There are physical accompanying sounds that are an essential part of movement — heart beat, breath rhythm, the noise of feet on the ground, body on the ground or in contact with others. The most obvious of these are stamping, clapping or even the gentler sound of touch in grasping and holding. Clothing, a clear example is the grass skirt, or personal decoration in the form of bangles or beads may all contribute a sound accompaniment that the dance would be the poorer without. Bells round the legs of English Morris men and African tribesmen are only one step removed from this, and from there one may follow an increasingly sophisticated trail of sound through a range of pitched and unpitched implements and instruments, to the point where the dancer is no longer able to support and play his instrument at the same time as move, and the sound comes from a source outside the dancer.

Being part of the body itself, the most natural musical instrument we have is the human voice. It is also the most

12

versatile and subtle sound source that exists. In addition to creating an endless variety of undifferentiated sounds, including grunts and shouts in primitive dancing, it can also load each of these with particular meaning and emotion by alterations of tone, pitch and volume before any actual language is needed. By itself it is an expressive medium and particularly so in alteration of musical tone and pitch which creates song.

The moment words are used, we have a further mode of expression. Vocal sound develops in two directions, musically into singing and linguistically through the use of words, although physically there is little difference in the production technicalities of either. Vocal sound is a part of movement, springing essentially from use of the body and its faculties.

For primitive man language was first of all a functional means of communication as he fought for day to day existence and the continuation of the species. As we find today, the sound would have been instinctively combined with sign-language — gestures and actions both mimetic and symbolic, as well as movements qualitatively supporting our statements. The need then would have been for maximum clarity in this sphere to aid the slowly developing linguistic abilities. Now, as then, non-verbal means of communication throw far more light on a matter in hand than is generally realised. The spoken word can deceive with immense facility.

Today in those languages which are the oldest and the most widely used there is incalcuable choice of words, sentence construction and nuance. This is the result of the migration of tribes and the intermingling of different forms of speech, and the continuous need for language to keep pace with new discoveries. Alongside this came the development of writing. Certain modes of writing are more functional than expressive, such as the recording of figures and information. On the creative side come narrative and descriptive prose, the essay, the novel, the play and the poem.

The words of the poem are symbols for the inspiration of the poet. Those words have generally accepted meanings or functions, but in addition they have certain secondary characteristics which are visual, aural and sometimes kinesthetic (or physically experienced). These characteristics are

13

often intensified through being combined in the chosen pattern or format of the poem. When written, poetry reaches the recipient in one of three ways: it may be read silently, spoken aloud or it may be heard. Each is a particular vehicle for secondary characteristics of the words, respectively a visual, kinesthetic or a solely aural stimulus is received in addition to the message of the poem.

Movement is kinesthetically experienced by the dancer in the flow of weight in time and space. It is visually experienced by the onlooker, though as a result of this he may also experience a diminished but reflected bodily sensation. Many of us have involuntarily jerked upwards as we have watched a dancer suddenly leap. Both the kinesthetic and the visual experience contribute to general movement understanding.

In combining poetry with creative dance or movement it must be remembered that both are art forms in their own right. A dancer has no need of a poet and the poet has no need of the dancer. Both can communicate directly with others without need of any other medium than the moving body or the spoken or written word, and because both are complete in themselves, totally contained within the structure of their own possibilities and limitations, both give the artist a chance to embody a statement peculiar to that medium alone. The more each form of art is explored, used and understood, the deeper we enable our consciousness to interpret the whole of life around us. Kant said "Perception without conception is blind, conception without perception empty".

Educational Development

The young child's reaction to his own ability to move and to utter sounds is enhanced by the excitement of discovery. New movement skills and words are repetitively indulged in first for the pleasurable experience of their performance and then for the satisfaction of the results. Both functionally and creatively this trying and testing of raw material takes place within each new field of human experience with continuing complexity. It is widened through the thinking process and becomes increasingly directed to chosen ends.

14

Movement education follows the natural process initiated by the intimate discovery of what parts of the body are there to be moved. Exploration of effort follows naturally — the time taken, the ground and space used and how the flow of body weight is involved. Movement relationships with others are explored between individuals and between groups. The whole follows the maturing process of the child himself. His spontaneous movement becomes enriched through heightened awareness of the capabilities of the body while his creative movement becomes a more meaningful selection of kinesthetically and visually known components.

With language the child first of all comes to master the mother tongue in order to express his needs. The physical and mental pleasure of arranging words in interesting sequences first of all meaningful to himself and finally to other people, is the first step towards realising the nature of language as an art form. Here also both the functional and the expressive go hand in hand in the learning process.

Poetry is a particularly specialised use of language, its writing requiring intimate knowledge of the 'feel' of words and their arrangements as well as understanding of connotation and content. Language education therefore first of all includes every conceivable situation in which children can talk, sing, act and listen, utilising both the producing and receiving of words. Because reading and writing are visual, the eye also needs to be involved in the appreciation of pictures, symbols and patterns so that later the making of word patterns follows easily. The heightened sensations produced by the rhythm and structure of a poem, in addition to the impact of its content, can make a lasting impression on a child.

Poetry is perhaps one of the most satisfying of stimuli to use with dance. However, its selection and use needs care. Not all poetry is suitable, and the chosen poem should be appropriate to the age and capabilities of the class. The individual teacher is the only judge of which poem will be successful with a particular class but certain types of poetry may be more applicable with one age group than another.

Infants and young juniors enjoy shorter more lively and direct poems. At this stage they are unable to interact in a structured way with other children, and so the emphasis will be on individual participation. Movement ideas can be suggested by the action of the subject or the descriptive words found in the poem; clear contrasts of size, shape, speed and tension will be most easily experienced.

As the children's scope widens they should be capable of using longer poems and those that demand group work. They will enjoy both directly narrative or 'pictorial' poems and those that express simple values. Using a poem, as the link, movement can often be incorporated into the project work undertaken by this age group. The inclusion of dance can enliven an integrated programme and it is a pity that this possibility is all too often neglected. This group will also enjoy nonsense poems and those with a strong rhythm or an onomatopoeic effect.

As the children mature the translation process can become more abstract. Older groups will enjoy poems that are intellectually demanding or thought-provoking. Some of the poems included are open-ended, others are controversial and these will stimulate discussion with more able groups. The added interest of translation into movement often singles out the pertinent issues, and it is sometimes within the dance medium that possible solutions are found. While older groups will not need the movement ideas to be spelled out to them they could nevertheless enjoy the challenge of undertaking demanding movement descriptions found in certain poems.

Practical Application

Once a poem has been selected, thought should be given to the aspect of the work which can best be interpreted in dance. The important aspect could be the subject matter. The poem could describe a vivid character, an exciting situation or an unexpected series of events. It could be concerned with a certain state of mind, an unusual idea, or embody a moral value. The poem might be of particular interest because the author has expressed attitudes with which one is sympathetic or because he introduces a new approach to the topic.

Alternatively the subject matter could be subordinate to the overall rhythm of the work or to the strong atmosphere it creates. Either of these aspects could be developed in movement. A further possible aspect could be the movement of the subject. The poet might describe the movements in detail, or with his skilful choice of words enable the reader to conjure up vividly the activity of the subject.

These aspects of the poem, subject matter, rhythm, atmosphere and movement are closely linked and interdependent. The whole structure and content of the poem will contribute indirectly to the resulting movement or dance, but it will help the teacher if he has selected which aspect of the poem he wishes to stress. This will help to clarify both his approach and the work of the group. The same poem could be treated in a number of different ways with various aspects predominating. It would not be surprising to find classes of widely differing age and experience tackling the same poem to very diverse ends.

Just as the total poem will contribute to the final dance composition, so the whole range of movement experience will be drawn upon. An appropriate use of all aspects of movement will be incorporated; body management, effort content, use of space and both individual and group work. Again, similar to the suggested choice of an aspect of the poem, it is of value to select definite movement themes. We have now reached the most important consideration in combining poetry with dance; the translation of the chosen aspect of the poem into selected movement ideas. This translation is the vital link in the work.

Some specific examples may help to clarify the translation process. If the poem describes two different characters such as a witch and a goblin, movements must be selected which both express the sentiments of the poem and lend themselves to show the contrast between the characters. The witch could be shown with slow sinuous movements, while the goblin could use quick angular movement. These ideas would be the main movement stress, but other ideas would also need to be considered, such as body shape and use of the hands and feet. The group shape could be linked — perhaps with the witches using circles and the goblins travelling in files. If the notion behind the poem was "attitude to greed" the main movement stress could be gathering and scattering. Use of tension and space might need to be brought in, and group ideas could develop from varying the placing of a focus.

To reiterate the translation process: having chosen the poem and selected which aspect is to be stressed, the teacher decides on the movement idea that would be most appropriately expressive. This forms the main movement theme (s) which is explored and developed fully. Laban's sixteen themes incorporating and expounding his principles of movement are a rich source of inspiration for dance teaching. They include simple principles relevant to beginners, and develop systematically through to a very advanced level. It is always valuable to incorporate a contrast or certain clear variations in a main movement theme. Long periods of movement work containing little variety are difficult to sustain in all but very experienced groups. The teacher will next add to the core movement idea other movement aspects that will serve both to reinforce the main theme and to develop other facets of the poem.

Work with a poem may lead to small group compositions or perhaps result in a whole class production. Alternatively its use may not result in any finished piece, but rather serve as an aid to movement awareness and exploration. Some obvious examples of this type of poem will be found in the anthology in the form of short fragments. Although it is realised that the poem will guide and feed the dance it is also true that it may tend to distract from the movement study. A high standard of work and full involvement in the movement are essential, and for this reason it is not always best to introduce the poem at the very beginning of the session. A short period of preoccupation with the movement theme (s) before the poem is introduced can be of great benefit to the final composition.

The final consideration is how best to present the movement in a composition. Dependent on the nature of the poem and its contents the work may develop as a solo, or ideas may be shown to advantage in pair or trio studies. Larger groups may dance alone or interlock as parts within the whole, or the entire group may form a "choir" dancing in unity of movement or design. Apart from intentionally individual work the final composition is often a combination of any or all of these. Group movement, shape and relationship are more expressive and satisfying then many teachers realise. A group in unison turning against itself, a group quick to follow any leader among its num-

18

ber, a group that is continously splitting up into smaller groups, only to reform again – all these can be strongly expressive. Further possibilities arise when groups work in relation to other groups: exciting visual patterns emerge, and the participation in a larger composition enriches the experience of the dancers.

In preparing the work, therefore, the teacher should know clearly his movement themes and have some idea as to how the movement could be developed individually, and integrated into a final whole. However, throughout the work he should be receptive and flexible with regard to the suggestions of the dancers themselves. The class should be given ample opportunity to experiment freely with the movement ideas and to discuss the interpretation and translation of the poem. It is often exciting to watch two groups working from the same starting point develop along very different lines. Assessment of each other's final results is most valuable, and the discussion may become usefully analytic and profound. There should never be any disparity between dance and poetry if they are used together, but rather there should be mutual enrichment. This enrichment will occur both while the class is moving and during discussion.

It will be seen from the notes on some of the poems at the end of the book that certain approaches are suggested. Terms such as dance drama, dramatic dance, symbolic interpretation and mime are mentioned and it may be helpful to clarify these.

In mime the posture and gestures of a person are imitated. They may be selected or adapted for dramatic effect. Adaptation could take the form of exaggeration of their effort content or of enlargement of their spatial characteristics. Sections of mime can well be included in a drama where a story line has to be communicated; they can also serve as starting points from which more dancelike activities develop. They may play a clear part in setting a scene or putting across an idea. The use of obvious working actions in a dance falls into this last category.

Mime in dance is confined to imitating people and occasionally animals, and should never include "being" an inanimate object. If the movement of a tree or a feather is being used the dance should move from a mimetic approach to a more symbolic one. There is little value in pretending to be a tree or a feather, but much benefit is gained from exploring in one's body the effort quality, the shape, or the type of movement that is significant in the chosen stimulus. Here we have the key to the symbolic approach. The important movement aspect of the stimulus is translated into dance and exploited fully by the dancer. The stimulus is the starting point and the guiding thread, but it is really the movement that is the chief preoccupation. The individual's movement, his relationship to others and the group formations all express, for example, the restless flexibility of the river or the intricate patterns of the snowflake.

If the symbolic idea is dramatic, perhaps concerned with an attitude, a mood or a single character the approach becomes one of dramatic dance; but as soon as the dance begins to have a sequence of events or a story to tell the work becomes a dance drama. In symbolic dance, mimetic actions have practically no place, however, in dance drama movement developed from mime is often used. The appropriate expressive aspects of a mimetic action may be stressed to such an extent that the movement is no longer mime. A lost and fearful person might take up a more curled posture and perform many more apprehensive groping gestures than could ever be seen in real life.

There is no clearly defined line between any of these types of dance, nor is it necessary to keep to one area within any one piece of work. The interpretation of a poem may ask for more than one approach, the inclusion of a moment of mime within a more symbolic composition may add significance to the idea being expressed. Notwithstanding it is advisable to know which approach is being employed in any part of the work to avoid muddled results.

Fantasy

THE RIDE-BY-NIGHTS

Up on their brooms the Witches stream,
Crooked and black in the crescent's gleam;
One foot high, and one foot low,
Bearded, cloaked, and cowled, they go.
'Neath Charlie's Wain they twitter and tweet,
And away they swarm 'neath the Dragon's feet,
With a whoop and a flutter they swing and sway,
And surge pell-mell down the Milky Way.
Between the legs of the glittering Chair
They hover and squeak in the empty air.
Then round they swoop past the glimmering Lion
To where Sirius barks behind huge Orion;
Up, then, and over to wheel amain
Under the silver, and home again.

WALTER DE LA MARE

THE WITCH

Weary went the old Witch,
Weary of her pack,
She sat her down by the churchyard wall,
And jerked it off her back.

The cord brake, yes, the cord brake,
Just where the dead did lie,
And Charms and Spells and Sorceries
Spilled out beneath the sky.

Weary was the old Witch;
She rested her old eyes
From the lantern-fruited yew trees,
And the scarlet of the skies;

And out the dead came stumbling,
From every rift and crack,
Silent as moss, and plundered
The gaping pack.

They wish them, three times over,
Away they skip full soon:
Bat and Mole and Leveret,
Under the rising moon;

Owl and Newt and Nightjar:
They take their shapes and creep
Silent as churchyard lichen,
While she squats asleep.

All of these dead were stirring:
Each unto each did call,
'A Witch, a Witch is sleeping
Under the churchyard wall;

'A Witch, a Witch is sleeping . . .'
The shrillness ebbed away;

And up the way-worn moon clomb bright,
Hard on the track of day.

She shone, high, wan, and silvery;
Day's colours paled and died:
And, save the mute and creeping worm,
Nought else was there beside.

Names may be writ; and mounds rise;
Purporting, Here be bones:
But empty is that churchyard
Of all save stones.

Owl and Newt and Nightjar,
Leveret, Bat, and Mole
Haunt and call in the twilight
Where she slept, poor soul.

WALTER DE LA MARE

UNWELCOME

We were young, we were merry, we were very very wise,
  And the door stood open at our feast,
When there passed us a woman with the West in her eyes,
  And a man with his back to the East.

O, still grew the hearts that were beating so fast,
  The loudest voice was still.
The jest died away on our lips as they passed,
  And the rays of July struck chill.

The cups of red wine turn'd pale on the board,
  The white bread black as soot.
The hound forgot the hand of her lord,
  She fell down at his foot.

Low let me lie, where the dead dog lies,
  Ere I sit me down again at a feast,
When there passes a woman with the West in her eyes,
  And a man with his back to the East.

MARY COLERIDGE

THE THREE WITCHES

First Witch	:	When shall we three meet again,
		In thunder, lightning, or in rain?
Second Witch	:	When the hurlyburly's done,
		When the battle's lost and won.
Third Witch	:	That will be ere the set of sun.
First Witch	:	Where the place?
Second Witch	:	Upon the heath.

*   *   *

First Witch	:	Thrice the brinded cat hath mew'd.

Second Witch	:	Thrice; and once the hedge-pig whin'd.
Third Witch	:	Harper cries? — 'tis time, 'tis time.
First Witch	:	Round about the cauldron go;
		In the poison'd entrails throw.
		Toad, that under cold stone,
		Days and nights hast thirty-one
		Swelter'd venom sleeping got,
		Boil thou first i' the charmed pot.
All	:	Double, double toil and trouble;
		Fire, burn; and, cauldron, bubble.
Second Witch	:	Fillet of a fenny snake,
		In the cauldron boil and bake;
		Eye of newt, and toe of frog,
		Wool of bat, and tongue of dog,
		Adder's fork, and blind-worm's sting,
		Lizard's leg, and owlet's wing,
		For a charm of powerful trouble,
		Like a hell-broth boil and bubble.
All	:	Double, double toil and trouble;
		Fire, burn; and, cauldron, bubble.
Third Witch	:	Scale of dragon; tooth of wolf;
		Witches' mummy; maw and gulf
		Of the ravin'd salt-sea shark;
		Root of hemlock, digg'd i' the dark;
		Liver of blaspheming Jew;
		Gall of goat; and slips of yew,
		Sliver'd in the moon's eclipse;
		Nose of Turk; and Tartar's lips;
		Finger of birth-strangled babe,
		Ditch-delivered by a drab,
		Make the gruel thick and slab:
		Add thereto a tiger's chaudron,
		For the ingredients of our cauldron.
All	:	Double, double toil and trouble;
		Fire, burn; and, cauldron, bubble.

W. SHAKESPEARE

SPACE TRAVELLERS

There was a witch, hump-backed and hooded,
Lived by herself in a burnt-out tree.
When the storm winds shrieked and the moon was buried
And the dark of the forest was black as black,
She rose in the air like a rocket at sea,
Riding the wind,
Riding the night,
Riding the tempest to the moon and back.

There may be a man with a hump of silver,
Telescope eyes and a telephone ear,
Dials to twist and knobs to twiddle,
Waiting for a night when skies are clear
To shoot from the scaffold with a blazing track,
Riding the dark,
Riding the cold,
Riding the silence to the moon and back.

JAMES NIMMO

The Sky

THE NATURE OF MATTER AND ENERGY

A sphere, which is as many thousand spheres,
Solid as crystal, yet through all its mass
Flow, as through empty space, music and light:
Ten thousand orbs involving and involved,
Purple and azure, white, and green, and golden,
Sphere within sphere; and every shape between
Peopled with unimaginable shapes,
Such as ghosts dream dwell in the lampless deep,
Yet each inter-transpicuous, and they whirl
Over each other with a thousand motions,
Upon a thousand sightless axles spinning,
And with the force of self-destroying swiftness,
Intensely, slowly, solemnly roll on.

PERCY BYSSHE SHELLEY

FIREWORKS

They rise like sudden fiery flowers
That burst upon the night,
Then fall to earth in burning showers
Of crimson, blue and white.

Like buds too wonderful to name,
Each miracle unfolds,
And catherine-wheels begin to flame
Like whirling marigolds.

Rockets and Roman candles make
An orchard of the sky,
Whence magic trees their petals shake
Upon each gazing eye.

JAMES REEVES

FOURTH OF JULY NIGHT

The little boat at anchor
in black water sat murmuring
to the tall black sky
      * * *

  A white sky bomb fizzed on a black line.
  A rocket hissed its red signature into the west.
  Now a shower of Chinese fire alphabets,
  a cry of flower pots broken in flames,
  a long curve to a purple spray,
  three violet balloons—
      Drips of seaweed tangled in gold,
      shimmering symbols of mixed numbers,
      tremulous arrangements of cream gold folds
      of a bride's wedding gown—

      * * *

A few sky bombs spoke their pieces,
then velvet dark.

The little boat at anchor
in black water sat murmuring
to the tall black sky.

CARL SANDBURG

TEA IN A SPACE-SHIP

In this world a tablecloth need not be laid
On any table, but is spread out anywhere
Upon the always equidistant and
Invisible legs of gravity's wild air.

The tea, which never would grow cold,
Gathers itself into a wet and steaming ball,
And hurls its liquid molecules at anybody's head,
Or dances, eternal bilboquet,
In and out of the suspended cups up—
Ended in the weightless hands
Of chronically nervous jerks
Who yet would never spill a drop,
Their mouths agape for passing cakes.

Lumps of sparkling sugar
Sling themselves out of their crystal bowl
With a disordered fountain's
Ornamental stops and starts.
The milk describes a permanent parabola
Girdled with satellites of spinning tarts.

The future lives with graciousness.
The hostess finds her problems eased,
For there is honey still for tea
And butter keeps the ceiling greased.

She will provide, of course,
No cake-forks, spoons or knives.
They are so sharp, so dangerously gadabout,
It is regarded as a social misdemeanour
To put them out.

JAMES KIRKUP

29

Weather

THE SNOWFLAKE

Before I melt,
Come, look at me!
This lovely icy filigree!
Of a great forest
In one night
I make a wilderness
Of white:
By skyey cold
Of crystals made,
All softly, on
Your finger laid,
I pause, that you
My beauty see:
Breathe, and I vanish
Instantly.

WALTER DE LA MARE

LONDON SNOW

When men were all asleep the snow came flying,
In large white flakes falling on the city brown,
Stealthily and perpetually settling and loosely lying,
    Hushing the latest traffic of the drowsy town;
Deadening, muffling, stifling its murmurs failing;
Lazily and incessantly floating down and down:
    Silently sifting and veiling road, roof and railing;

Hiding difference, making unevenness even,
Into angles and crevices softly drifting and sailing.
    All night it fell, and when full inches seven
It lay in the depth of its uncompacted lightness,
The clouds blew off from a high and frosty heaven;
    And all woke earlier for the unaccustomed brightness
Of the winter dawning, the strange unheavenly glare:
The eye marvelled — marvelled at the dazzling whiteness;
    The ear hearkened to the stillness of the solemn air;
No sound of wheel rumbling nor of foot falling,
And the busy morning cries came thin and spare.
    Then boys I heard, as they went to school, calling,
They gathered up the crystal manna to freeze
Their tongues with tasting, their hands with snowballing;
    Or rioted in a drift, plunging up to the knees;
Or peering up from under the white-mossed wonder,
'O look at the trees!' they cried, 'O look at the trees!'
    With lessened load a few carts creak and blunder,
Following along the white deserted way,
A country company long dispersed asunder:
    When now already the sun, in pale display
Standing by Paul's high dome, spread forth below
His sparkling beams, and awoke the stir of the day.
    For now doors open, and war is waged with the snow;
And trains of sombre men, past tale of number,
Tread long brown paths, as toward their toil they go:
    But even for them awhile no cares encumber
Their minds diverted; the daily word is unspoken,
The daily thoughts of labour and sorrow slumber
At the sight of the beauty that greets them, for the charm
       they have broken.

ROBERT BRIDGES

FOG

The fog comes
on little cat feet.

It sits looking
over harbour and city
on silent haunches
and then moves on.

CARL SANDBURG

FOG

Curling and writhing, slowly
Enveloping all in its billowing mass, coldly,
Slowly it creeps on, and on,
Till none can see anything, but fog.

Slowly it descends, a cloud,
Upon a lawn, or city,
Making all look grey, and sad,
But it goes as it comes, slowly.

FRANCES HORNER

WILD IRON

Sea go dark, go dark with wind,
Feet go heavy, heavy with sand,
Thoughts go wild, wild with the sound
Of iron on the old shed swinging, clanging:
Go dark, go heavy, go wild, go round,
    Dark with the wind,
    Heavy with the sand,
Wild with the iron that tears at the nail,
And the foundering shriek of the gale.

ALLEN CURNOW

32

STORM IN THE BLACK FOREST

Now it is almost night, from the bronzey soft sky
jugful after jugful of pure white liquid fire, bright white
tipples over and spills down,
and is gone
and gold-bronze flutters beat through the thick upper air.

And as the electric liquid pours out, sometimes
a still brighter white snake wriggles among it, spilled
and tumbling wriggling down the sky:
and then the heavens cackle with uncouth sounds.

And the rain won't come, the rain refuses to come!

This is the electricity that man is supposed to have mastered
chained, subjugated to his own use!

supposed to!

D. H. LAWRENCE

AN AWFUL TEMPEST

An awful tempest mashed the air
The clouds were gaunt and few;
A black, as of a spectre's cloak
Hid heaven and earth from view.

The creatures chuckled on the roofs
And whistled in the air,
And shook their fists and gnashed their teeth,
And swung their frenzied hair.

The morning lit, the birds arose;
The monster's faded eyes
Turned slowly to his native coast,
And peace was Paradise!

EMILY DICKINSON

33

Water

THE SONG OF THE RIVER

Clear and cool, clear and cool,
By laughing shallow, and dreaming pool;
Cool and clear, cool and clear,
By shining shingle, and foaming wear;
Under the crag where the ouzel sings,
And the ivied wall where the church-bell rings,
Undefiled, for the undefiled;
Play by me, bathe in me, mother and child.

Dank and foul, dank and foul,
By the smoky town in its murky cowl;
Foul and dank, foul and dank,
By wharf and sewer and slimy bank;
Darker and darker the farther I go,
Baser and baser the richer I grow;
Who dare sport with the sin-defiled?
Shrink from me, turn from me, mother and child.

Strong and free, strong and free,
The floodgates are open, away to the sea,
Free and strong, free and strong,
Cleansing my streams as I hurry along,
To the golden sands and the leaping bar,
And the taintless tide that awaits me afar.
As I lose myself in the infinite main,
Like a soul that has sinned and is pardoned again.
Undefiled, for the undefiled;
Play by me, bathe in me, mother and child.

CHARLES KINGSLEY

PORT OF HOLY PETER

The blue laguna rocks and quivers,
  Dull gurgling eddies twist and spin,
The climate does for people's livers,
  It's a nasty place to anchor in
     Is Spanish port,
     Fever port,
     Port of Holy Peter.

The town begins on the sea-beaches,
  And the town's mad with the stinging flies,
The drinking water's mostly leeches,
  It's a far remove from Paradise
     Is Spanish port,
     Fever port,
     Port of Holy Peter.

There's sand-bagging and throat-slitting,
  And quiet graves in the sea slime,
Stabbing, of course, and rum-hitting,
  Dirt, and drink, and stink, and crime,
     In Spanish port,
     Fever port,
     Port of Holy Peter.

All the day the wind's blowing
  From the sick swamp below the hills,
All the night the plague's growing,
  And the dawn brings the fever chills,
     In Spanish port,
     Fever port,
     Port of Holy Peter.

You get a thirst there's no slaking,
  You get the chills and fever-shakes,
Tongue yellow and head aching,
  And then the sleep that never wakes.
And all the year the heat's baking,
  The sea rots and the earth quakes,
        In Spanish port,
        Fever port,
        Port of Holy Peter.

JOHN MASEFIELD

THE SEA

The waves like ripples
Crumple
Against withering shores.
The dying foam retreats,
into the cluster of emerald greens.
Its emotional surface broken,
By quivering breezes.
Showing its freedom,
by violent tantrums that
beat feeble shores.
Then, going back into a tranquil
mood,
Almost accepting defeat.

M. J. JOSEY

36

THE WATER ZOO

To-day I have seen all I wish,
For I have seen four thousand fish,
*   Inscrutable and rum,*
Observing me with solemn eyes
That hold no anger or surprise,
*   In the Aquarium.*

Because they float about my brain,
To-morrow I should like to come,
And see four thousand fish again.

For there are pike and trout and carp,
And fish with faces long and sharp,
And wrasse with their mosaic scales,
And oblong fish that have no tails;
Fresh-water and soft-water fellows,
And fish with valves that work like bellows;
And fish that leap and fish that crawl,
And great octopodes a-sprawl,
Inside those aqueous mysteries
Below the Mappin Terraces;
And golden fish with filmy skirts
That move like Oriental flirts,
And rainbow-coloured fish that seem
Like sunsets dipped into a stream,
And silver fish with dusky bars
That float beneath the nenuphars,
The tiny fish of Paradise,

And fish with furry backs, like mice,
And fish that lay their eggs on land
By leaping, as I understand,
And placing them on grass, but yet
Must splash about to keep them wet;
The sea-hare, which is like a slug,
The wolf-fish with an awful mug,

And sharks with faces mild and prim,
Like schoolgirls, elegantly slim—
You would not dream that underneath
That tiny mouth had all those teeth—
And humorous turtles that advance
As though in some Salome dance,
And hermit crabs that have the sense
To use a whelk-shell residence
To walk about within the sea,
Whereon there sprouts, most luckily,
A poisonous anemone.

And there are fish that kiss and climb,
And fish that croak, though not in rhyme,
And sucking-fish that hang on rocks,
And eels that give electric shocks,
And fish that turn a rosy pink,
From sheer false modesty, I think—
And fish that, floating on the tide,
Transparent, show their whole inside;
Not ray-fish these, but, should you wish,
They may be termed the X-ray fish;
And flat fish with their eyes askew,
All buried, save those eyes, from view
Beneath the clean white sand, until
With rippling movements they ascend
To eat some portion of a friend
Thrown in by keepers from the top;
And fish that always seem to stop

Lying in one place, dull as lead,
Although you tap quite near their head;
And salamanders dark and dire,
And axolotls, whose desire
To be a salamander fills
Their bosom with ecstatic thrills;
But no — the awful hand of Fate

Prevents them from that longed-for state.
For grow to be a salamander
(Though striving with uncommon candour
And patient as a nurse or aunt)
The axolotl simply can't;
Because of his peculiar gland
He may not hope to salamand;
His life's ambition forced to throttle,
He still remains an axolotl.
And there the crayfish or *langouste*
On craggy rocks is seen to roost. . . .

> *To-day I have seen all I wish,*
> *For I have seen four thousand fish,*
> *   Inscrutable and rum,*
> *Observing me with solemn eyes*
> *That hold no anger or surprise,*
> *   In the Aquarium.*
>
> *Because they float about my brain,*
> *To-morrow I should like to come*
> *And see four thousand fish again.*

EVOE

THE CATARACT OF LODORE

The cataract strong
Then plunges along,
Striking and raging
As if a war waging
Its caverns and rocks among:
Rising and leaping,
Sinking and creeping,
Swelling and sweeping,
Showering and springing,
Flying and flinging,
Writhing and ringing,
Eddying and whisking,
Spouting and frisking,
Twining and twisting,
    Around and around
    With endless rebound!
Smiting and fighting,
A sight to delight in;
Confounding, astounding,
Dizzying and deafening the ear with its sound.
Collecting, projecting,
Receding and speeding,
And shocking and rocking,
And darting and parting,
And threading and spreading,
And whizzing and hissing,
And dripping and skipping,
And hitting and splitting,
And shining and twining,
And rattling and battling,
And shaking and quaking,
And pouring and roaring,
And waving and raving,
And tossing and crossing,

And flowing and going,
And running and stunning,
And foaming and roaming,

And dinning and spinning
And dropping and hopping,
And working and jerking,
And guggling and struggling,
And heaving and cleaving,
And moaning and groaning;

And glittering and frittering,
And gathering and feathering,
And whitening and brightening,
And quivering and shivering,
And hurrying and skurrying,
And thundering and floundering;
Dividing and gliding and sliding,
And falling and crawling and sprawling,
And driving and riving and striving,
And sprinkling and twinkling and wrinkling,
And sounding and bounding and rounding,
And bubbling and troubling and doubling,
And grumbling and rumbling and tumbling,
And clattering and battering and shattering;

Retreating and beating and meeting and sheeting,
Delaying and straying and playing and spraying,
Advancing and prancing and glancing and dancing,
Recoiling, turmoiling and toiling and boiling,
And gleaming and steaming and streaming and beaming,
And rushing and flushing and brushing and gushing,
And flapping and rapping and clapping and slapping,
And curling and whirling and purling and twirling,
And thumping and plumping and bumping and jumping,
And dashing and flashing and splashing and clashing;
And so never ending, but always descending,

Sounds and motions for ever and ever are blending,
All at once and all o'er, with mighty uproar,
And this way the Water comes down at Lodore.

ROBERT SOUTHEY

The Countryside

THE LAND

A hundred thousand million years ago
The land was hot
And empty;
Covered
By molten metals, and the
Sluggish sea, crawling over
Slow-cooling granite.
   And from that barren skin of
Ancient shapes, the mighty Sculptor
Carved out valleys, raised up
Crumbling hills, and
Broke them
Violently apart, lifting fiery fountains
From the sea.
   Then
Were many mighty mountains made;
And the wrinkled skin of land
Still lies, pitted
And disfigured;
Ever changing.

CELIA MAYES

RAIN ON DRY GROUND

That is rain on dry ground. We heard it:
We saw the little tempest in the grass,
The panic of anticipation: heard
The uneasy leaves flutter, the air pass
In a wave, the fluster of the vegetation;

Heard the first spatter of drops, the outriders
Larruping on the road, hitting against
The gate of the drought, and shattering
On to the lances of the tottering meadow.
It is rain; it is rain on dry ground.

Rain riding suddenly out of the air,
Battering the bare walls of the sun.
It is falling on to the tongue of the blackbird,
Into the heart of the thrush; the dazed valley
Sings it down. Rain, rain on dry ground!

This is the urgent decision of the day,
The urgent drubbing of earth, the urgent raid
On the dust; downpour over the flaring poppy,
Deluge on the face of noon, the flagellant
Rain drenching across the air. — The day

Flows in the ditch; bubble and twisting twig
And the sodden morning swirl along together
Under the crying hedge. And where the sun
Ran on the scythes, the rain runs down
The obliterated field, the blunted crop.

> The rain stops.
> The air is sprung with green.
> The intercepted drops
> Fall at their leisure; and between
> The threading runnels on the slopes
> The snail drags his caution into the sun.

CHRISTOPHER FRY

HUMMING-BIRD

I can imagine, in some otherworld
Primeval-dumb, far back
In that most awful stillness, that only gasped and hummed,
Humming-birds raced down the avenues.

Before anything had a soul,
While life was a heave of Matter, half inanimate,
This little bit chipped off in brilliance
And went whizzing through the slow, vast, succulent
        stems.

I believe there were no flowers then,
In the world where the humming-bird flashed ahead of
        creation.
I believe he pierced the slow vegetable veins with his
        long beak.

Probably he was big
As mosses, and little lizards, they say, were once big.
Probably he was a jabbing, terrifying monster.

We look at him through the wrong end of the long
        telescope of Time,
Luckily for us.

D. H. LAWRENCE

BARE ALMOND-TREES

Wet almond-trees, in the rain,
Like iron sticking grimly out of earth;
Black almond trunks, in the rain,
Like iron implements twisted, hideous, out of the earth,
Out of the deep, soft fledge of Sicilian winter-green,
Earth-grass uneatable,

44

Almond trunks curving blackly, iron-dark, climbing the
    slopes.

Almond-tree, beneath the terrace rail,
Black, rusted, iron trunk,
You have welded your thin stems finer,
Like steel, like sensitive steel in the air,
Grey, lavender, sensitive steel, curving thinly and brittly
    up in a parabola.

What are you doing in the December rain?
Have you a strange electric sensitiveness in your steel tips?
Do you feel the air for electric influences
Like some strange magnetic apparatus?
Do you take in messages, in some strange code,
From heaven's wolfish, wandering electricity, that prowls
    so constantly round Etna?
Do you take the whisper of sulphur from the air?
Do you hear the chemical accents of the sun?
Do you telephone the roar of the waters over the earth?
And from all this, do you make calculations?

Sicily, December's Sicily in a mass of rain
With iron branching blackly, rusted like old, twisted
    implements
And brandishing and stooping over earth's wintry fledge,
    climbing the slopes
Of uneatable soft green!

D. H. LAWRENCE

Machines

THE EXPRESS

After the first powerful plain manifesto
The black statement of pistons, without more fuss
But gliding like a queen, she leaves the station.
Without bowing and with restrained unconcern
She passes the houses which humbly crowd outside,
The gasworks and at last the heavy page
Of death, printed by gravestones in the cemetery.
Beyond the town there lies the open country
Where, gathering speed, she acquires mystery,
The luminous self-possession of ships on ocean.
It is now she begins to sing — at first quite low
Then loud, and at last with a jazzy madness —
The song of her whistle screaming at curves,
Of deafening tunnels, brakes, innumerable bolts.
And always light, aerial underneath,
Goes the elate metre of her wheels.
Steaming through metal landscape on her lines
She plunges new eras of wild happiness
Where speed throws up strange shapes, broad curves
And parallels clean like the steel of guns.
At last, further than Edinburgh or Rome,
Beyond the crest of the world, she reaches night
Where only a low streamline brightness
Of phosphorus on the tossing hills is white.
Ah, like a comet through flame she moves entranced
Wrapt in her music no bird song, no, nor bough
Breaking with honey buds, shall ever equal.

STEPHEN SPENDER

46

THE AMERICAN RAILWAY

In eighteen hundred and eighty-one
The American Railway was begun,
In eighteen hundred and eighty-one,
Working on the railway.

In eighteen hundred and eighty-two
I found myself with nothing to do,
In eighteen hundred and eighty-two,
But work upon the railway.

In eighteen hundred and eighty-three
The overseer accepted me,
In eighteen hundred and eighty-three,
To work upon the railway.

In eighteen hundred and eighty-four
My hands were tired and my feet were sore,
In eighteen hundred and eighty-four,
With working on the railway.

In eighteen hundred and eighty-five
I found myself more dead than alive,
In eighteen hundred and eighty-five,
Through working on the railway.

In eighteen hundred and eighty-six
I trod on a box of dynamite sticks,
In eighteen hundred and eighty-six,
Working on the railway.

In eighteen hundred and eighty-seven
I found myself on the way to heaven,
In eighteen hundred and eighty-seven,
Working on the railway.

In eighteen hundred and eighty-eight
I found myself at the Golden Gate

In eighteen hundred and eighty-eight,
Working on the railway.

In eighteen hundred and eighty-nine
A cherub's harp and wings were mine,
In eighteen hundred and eighty-nine,
Above the American railway.

In eighteen hundred and eighty-ten
If you want any more we will sing it again,
In eighteen hundred and eighty-ten,
Working on the railway.

ANON

LINES

Straight lines, long lines,
Curved lines, short lines,
Thick lines, thin lines,
Horizontal, vertical,
Parallel and spiral,
Diagonal and zig-zag,
All sorts of lines.

Lines for the telephone, if they cross you're in a mess,
Good strong life-lines for people in distress.
Nylon lines for fishing, don't forget the bait,
Plumb lines to hang down to see if things are straight.
Hundreds of white lines down the middle of the road,
If you don't know about yellow lines, read the Highway Code.

Railway lines, clothes lines,
Write out hundred times lines!
Lines about us all the time,
All sorts of lines.

DEBORAH BESTWICK

GENERATOR

Close shut
Behind high voltage doors
Of council green
Drones the quiet monotone,
Wary and watchful
And supremely self-contained.

Manacled deep within a concrete cage
Gleams the smug, oily, leering
Of contorted pipes
Squatting contented in the throbbing gloom
And gloating like a fat gunmetal fly,
Obscene and sleek,
Gorged on a carcase of electric power.

GLENIS SYME

THE SECRET OF THE MACHINES

We were taken from the ore-bed and the mine,
   We were melted in the furnace and the pit —
We were cast and wrought and hammered to design,
   We were cut and filed and tooled and gauged to fit.
Some water, coal, and oil is all we ask,
   And a thousandth of an inch to give us play,
And now if you will set us to our task,
   We will serve you four and twenty hours a day!

   We can pull and haul and push and lift and drive,
   We can print and plough and weave and heat and light,
   We can run and jump and swim and fly and dive,
   We can see and hear and count and read and write!

Would you call a friend from half across the world?
   If you'll let us have his name and town and state,

You shall see and hear your crackling question hurled
    Across the arch of heaven while you wait.
Has he answered? Does he need you at his side?
    You can start this very evening if you choose,
And take the Western Ocean in the stride
    Of thirty thousand horses and some screws!

    The boat-express is waiting your command!
    You will find the *Mauretania* at the quay,
    Till her captain turns the lever 'neath his hand,
    And the monstrous nine-decked city goes to sea.

Do you wish to make the mountains bare their head
    And lay their new-cut forests at your feet?
Do you want to turn a river in its bed,
    And plant a barren wilderness with wheat?
Shall we pipe aloft and bring you water down
    From the never-failing cisterns of the snows,
To work the mills and tramways in your town,
    And irrigate your orchards as it flows?

    It is easy! Give us dynamite and drills!
    Watch the iron-shouldered rocks lie down and quake
    As the thirsty desert-level floods and fills,
    And the valley we have dammed becomes a lake!

But remember, please, the Law by which we live,
    We are not built to comprehend a lie,
We can neither love nor pity nor forgive,
    If you make a slip in handling us you die!
We are greater than the Peoples or the Kings—
    Be humble, as you crawl beneath our rods!—
Our touch can alter all created things,
    We are everything on earth — except the Gods!

    Though our smoke may hide the Heavens from your eyes,
    It will vanish and the stars will shine again,
    Because, for all our power and weight and size,
    We are nothing more than children of your brain!

RUDYARD KIPLING

People

PEOPLE

I like people quite well
at a little distance.
I like to see them passing and passing
and going their own way,
especially if I see their aloneness alive in them.
Yet I don't want them to come near.
If they will only leave me alone
I can still have the illusion that there is room enough in the
      world.

D. H. LAWRENCE

JINGLE

I am a poor man in a train,
I go to work and come again
And there is nothing in my brain
But go to work and come again.

I am a person in a crowd,
I cannot speak my thoughts aloud.
To the distinguished and the proud
I cannot speak my thoughts aloud.

I am a leader and my power
Can kill your leaders in an hour.
I am a poor man in a train,
I go to work and come again.

I am a person in a crowd,
I cannot speak my thoughts aloud.

PETER CHAMPKIN

THE MAN IN THE BOWLER HAT

I am the unnoticed, the unnoticeable man:
The man who sat on your right in the morning train:
The man you look through like a windowpane:
The man who was the colour of the carriage, the
                                    colour of the mounting
Morning pipe-smoke.

I am the man too busy with living to live,
Too hurried and worried to see and smell and touch:
The man who is patient too long and obeys too much
And wishes too softly and seldom.

I am the man they call the nation's backbone,
Who am boneless — playable catgut, pliable clay:
The Man they label Little lest one day
I dare to grow.

I am the rails on which the moment passes,
The megaphone for many words and voices:
I am graph, diagram,
Composite face.

I am the led, the easily-fed
The tool, the not-quite-fool,
The would-be-safe-and-sound,
The uncomplaining, bound,
The dust fine-ground,
Stone-for-a-statue waveworn pebble-round.

A.S.J. TESSIMOND

THE BRITISH

We are a people living in shells and moving
Crablike; reticent, awkward, deeply suspicious;
Watching the world from a corner of half-closed eyelids,
Afraid lest someone show that he hates or loves us,
Afraid lest someone weep in a railway train.

We are coiled and clenched like a foetus clad in armour.
We hold our hearts for fear they fly like eagles.
We grasp our tongues for fear they cry like trumpets.
We listen to our own footsteps. We look both ways
Before we cross the silent empty road.

We are a people easily made uneasy,
Especially wary of praise, of passion, of scarlet
Cloaks, of gesturing hands, of the smiling stranger
In the alien hat who talks to all or the other
In the unfamiliar coat who talks to none.

We are afraid of too-cold thought or too-hot
Blood, of the opening of long shut shafts or cupboards,
Of light in caves, of Xrays, probes, unclothing
Of emotion, intolerable revelation
Of lust in the light, of love in the palm of the hand.

We are afraid of, one day on a sunny morning,
Meeting ourselves or another without the usual
Outer sheath, the comfortable conversation.
And saying all, all, all we did not mean to,
All, all, all we did not know we meant.

A.S.J. TESSIMOND

MAGGIE AND MILLY AND MOLLY AND MAY

maggie and milly and molly and may
went down to the beach (to play one day)

and maggie discovered a shell that sang
so sweetly she couldn't remember her troubles, and

milly befriended a stranded star
whos rays five languid fingers were;

and molly was chased by a horrible thing
which raced sideways while blowing bubbles: and

may came home with a smooth round stone
as small as a world and as large as alone.

for whatever we lose (like a you or a me)
it's always ourselves we find in the sea

E.E. CUMMINGS

SMILING VILLAIN

Forth from his den to steal he stole,
His bags of chink he chunk,
And many a wicked smile he smole,
And many a wink he wunk.

ANON

WAGES

The wages of work is cash.
The wages of cash is want more cash.
The wages of want more cash is vicious competition.
The wages of vicious competition is — the world we live in.

The work-cash-want circle is the viciousest circle
that ever turned men into fiends.

Earning a wage is a prison occupation
and a wage-earner is a sort of gaol-bird.

Earning a salary is a prison overseer's job,
a gaoler instead of a gaol-bird.

Living on your income is strolling grandly outside the prison
in terror lest you have to go in. And since the work-prison
covers almost every scrap of the living earth, you stroll up and
down on a narrow beat, about the same as a prisoner taking
his exercise.

This is called universal freedom.

D. H. LAWRENCE

THE FEEL OF HANDS

The hands explore tentatively,
two small live entities whose shapes
I have to guess at. They touch me
all, with light of fingertips.

testing each surface of each thing
found, timid as kittens with it.
I connect them with amusing
hands I have shaken by daylight.

There is sudden transition:
they plunge together in a full
formed single fury; they are grown
to cats, hunting without scruple;

they are expert but desperate.
I am in the dark. I wonder
when they grew up. It strikes me that
I do not know whose hands they are.

THOM GUNN

CHOOSE

The single clenched fist, lifted and ready
Or the open asking hand, held out and waiting.
Choose.
For we meet by one or the other.

CARL SANDBURG

THE BUILDERS

Staggering slowly, and swaying
Heavily at each slow foot's lift and drag,
With tense eyes careless of the roar and throng,
That under jut and jag
Of half-built wall and scaffold streams along,
Six bowed men straining strong
Bear, hardly lifted, a huge lintel stone.
This ignorant thing and prone,
Mere dumbness, blindly weighing,
A brute piece of blank death, a bone
Of the stark mountain, helpless and inert,
Yet draws each sinew till the hot veins swell
And sweat-drops upon hand and forehead start,
Till with short pants the suffering heart
Throbs to the throat, where fiercely hurt
Crushed shoulders cannot heave; till thought and sense
Are nerved and narrowed to one aim intense,
One effort scarce to be supported longer!
What tyrant will in man or God were stronger
To summon, thrall and seize
The exaction of life's uttermost resource
That from the down-weighed breast and aching knees
To arms lifted in pain
And hands that grapple and strain,
Upsurges, thrusting desperate to repel
The pressure and the force
Of this, which neither feels, nor hears, nor sees?

LAURENCE BINYON

PRAYER BEFORE BIRTH

I am not yet born; O hear me.
Let not the bloodsucking bat or the rat or the stoat or the
    club-footed ghoul come near me.

I am not yet born; console me.
I fear that the human race may with tall walls wall me,
    with strong drugs dope me, with wise lies lure me,
        on black racks rack me, in blood-baths roll me.

I am not yet born; provide me
With water to dandle me, grass to grow for me, trees to talk
    to me, sky to sing to me, birds and a white light
        in the back of my mind to guide me.

I am not yet born; forgive me
For the sins that in me the world shall commit, my words
    when they speak me, my thoughts when they think me,
        my treason engendered by traitors beyond me,
            my life when they murder by means of my
                hands, my death when they live me.

I am not yet born; rehearse me
In the parts I must play and the cues I must take when
    old men lecture me, bureaucrats hector me, mountains
        frown at me, lovers laugh at me, the white
            waves call me to folly and the desert calls
                me to doom and the beggar refuses
                    my gift and my children curse me.

I am not yet born; O hear me,
Let not the man who is beast or who thinks he is God
    come near me.

I am not yet born; O fill me
With strength against those who would freeze my
    humanity, would dragoon me into a lethal automaton,
        would make me a cog in a machine, a thing with

one face, a thing, and against all those
who would dissipate my entirety, would
blow me like thistledown hither and
thither or hither and thither
like water held in the
hands would spill me.

Let them not make me a stone and let them not spill me.
Otherwise kill me.

LOUIS MACNEICE

Happenings

EZEKIEL

Ezekiel in the valley of Dry Bones
Heard the word of the Lord commanding him:
"Prophesy to these bones that they may live."
There was a noise and a shaking; and bone to bone
Clove together, and sinew and flesh came on them.

Yet there was no breath in them. The Lord commanded:
"Prophesy, Son of Man, to the four winds."
And the winds came from the corners of the earth,
Breathing upon those dead, and clothed in flesh
Was a great army standing upon their feet.

I dreamed I stood in a valley of dry bones.
But what were these? derelict, rusty, mounded
Clutter and offal of man's invention, dry bones
Cast aside by hurrying civilisation,
Yesterday's triumph, that To-day despises.

With a noise of hissing they were coming together.
Fire breathed on them, and metal clove to metal,
Timed and measured, each to its intricate function,
Minute or monstrous, all in the brain engendered,
Convolutions, multiplied over and over.

Panting and humming, forms combined to a meaning,
Usurping the sky, supplanting the sweet verdure,
Forms from the blinding furnace issuing, huge
Giantry of metal, dwarfing man to a pigmy,
Sounding, clamouring, throbbing in speed and power.

Proud we gaze on all we have mastered, — captive
Force, and willed conformity, stamped exactness.
But O divine diversity of creatures,
Where are you? Not here amid man's contrivings;
None can repeat you, none complete, not annul you.

LAURENCE BINYON

THE HAMMERS

Noise of hammers once I heard,
Many hammers, busy hammers,
Beating, shaping, night and day,
Shaping, beating dust and clay
To a palace; saw it reared;
Saw the hammers laid away.

And I listened, and I heard
Hammers beating, night and day,
In the palace newly reared,
Beating it to dust and clay:
Other hammers, muffled hammers,
Silent hammers of decay.

RALPH HODGSON

THE TERM

A rumpled sheet
of brown paper
about the length

and apparent bulk
of a man was
rolling with the

wind slowly over
and over in
the street as

a car drove down
upon it and
crushed it to

the ground. Unlike
a man it rose
again rolling

with the wind over
and over to be as
it was before.

W. C. WILLIAMS

EARTHQUAKE

An old man's flamingo-coloured kite
Twitches higher over tiled roofs.
Idly gazing through the metal gauze
That nets the winter sun beyond my sliding windows,
I notice that all the telegraph-poles along the lane
Are waggling convulsively, and the wires
Bounce like skipping-ropes round flustered birds.

62

The earth creeps under the floor. A cherry tree
Agitates itself outside, but it is no wind
That makes the long bamboo palisade
Begin to undulate down all its length.

The clock stammers and stops. There is a queer racket,
Like someone rapping on the wooden walls,
Then through the ceiling's falling flakes I see
The brass handles on a high chest of drawers
Dithering and dancing in a brisk distraction.
The lamp swings like a headache, and the whole house
Rotates slightly on grinding rollers.
Smoothly, like a spoilt child putting out a tongue,
A drawer shoots half-out, and quietly glides back again,
Closed with a snap of teeth, a sharper click
Than such a casual grimace prepared me for.

The stove-pipe's awkward elbow
Twangles its three supporting wires. Doors
Slam, fly open: my quiet maid erupts from
Nowhere, blushing furiously, yet smiling wildly
As if to explain, excuse, console and warn.
Together, like lost children in a fairy-tale
Who escape from an enchanter's evil cottage,
We rush out into the slightly unbalanced garden. A pole
Vibrates still like a plucked bass string,
But the ground no longer squirms beneath our feet,
And the trees are composing themselves, have birds again.

In the spooky quiet, a 'plane drones
Like a metal top, and though the sound
Gives a sense of disaster averted,
And is even oddly re-assuring, as
The pulse of confident engines,
Throbbing high above an electric storm, can comfort,
We feel that somewhere out of sight
Something has done its worst. Meanwhile

The house tries to look as if nothing had happened,
And over the roof's subtle curves
Lets the flamingo-coloured kite fly undisturbed.

JAMES KIRKUP

PEACE

Peace is written on the doorstep
In lava.

Peace, black peace congealed.
My heart will know no peace
Till the hill bursts.

Brilliant, intolerable lava,
Brilliant as a powerful burning-glass,
Walking like a royal snake down the mountain
        towards the sea.

Forests, cities, bridges
Gone again in the bright trail of lava.
Naxos thousands of feet below the olive-roots,
And now the olive leaves thousands of feet below
        the lava fire.

Peace congealed in black lava on the doorstep.
Within, white-hot lava, never at peace
Till it burst forth blinding, withering the earth;
To set again into rock,
Grey-black rock.

Call it Peace?

D. H. LAWRENCE

EVERYONE SANG

Everyone suddenly burst out singing;
And I was filled with such delight
As prisoned birds must find in freedom
Winging wildly across the white
Orchards and dark green fields; on; on; and out
     of sight

Everyone's voice was suddenly lifted,
And beauty came like the setting sun.
My heart was shaken with tears, and horror
Drifted away . . . O but every one
Was a bird; and the song was wordless; the
     singing will never be done.

SIEGFRIED SASSOON

BAT

At evening, sitting on this terrace,
When the sun from the west, beyond Pisa, beyond the
   mountains of Carrara
Departs, and the world is taken by surprise. . .

When the tired flower of Florence is in gloom beneath the
   glowing
Brown hills surrounding. . .

When under the arches of the Ponte Vecchio
A green light enters against stream, flush from the west,
Against the current of obscure Arno. . .

Look up, and you see things flying
Between the day and the night;
Swallows with spools of dark thread sewing the shadows
   together.

65

A circle swoop, and a quick parabola under the bridge
    arches
Where light pushes through;
A sudden turning upon itself of a thing in the air.
A dip to the water.

And you think:
'The swallows are flying so late!'

Swallows?

Dark air-life looping
Yet missing the pure loop. . .

A twitch, a twitter, an elastic shudder in flight
And serrated wings against the sky,
Like a glove, a black glove thrown up at the light,
And falling back.

Never swallows!
Bats!
The swallows are gone.

At a wavering instant the swallows give way to bats
By the Ponte Vecchio. . .
Changing guard.

Bats, and an uneasy creeping in one's scalp
As the bats sweep overhead!
Flying madly.

Pipistrello!
Black piper on an infinitesimal pipe.
Little lumps that fly in air and have voices indefinite, wildly
    vindictive;

Wings like bits of umbrella.

Bats!

Creatures that hang themselves up like an old rag, to sleep;
And disgustingly upside down.
Hanging upside down like rows of disgusting old rags
And grinning in their sleep.
Bats!

In China the bat is symbol of happiness.

Not for me!

D. H. LAWRENCE

Nonsense

THEY TOLD ME YOU HAD BEEN TO HER

'They told me you had been to her,
  And mentioned me to him:
She gave me a good character,
  But said I could not swim.

He sent them word I had not gone,
  (We know it to be true):
If she should push the matter on,
  What would become of you?

I gave her one, they gave him two,
  You gave us three or more;
They all returned from him to you,
  Though they were mine before.

If I or she should chance to be
  Involved in this affair,
He trusts to you to set them free,
  Exactly as we were.

My notion was that you had been
  (Before she had this fit)
An obstacle that came between
  Him, and ourselves, and it.

Don't let him know she liked them best,
  For this must ever be
A secret, kept from all the rest,
  Between yourself and me.'

LEWIS CARROLL

68

JABBERWOCKY

'Twas brillig, and the slithy toves
   Did gyre and gimble in the wabe;
All mimsy were the borogoves,
   And the mome raths outgrabe.

'Beware the Jabberwock, my son!
   The jaws that bite, the claws that catch!
Beware the Jubjub bird, and shun
   The frumious Bandersnatch!'

He took his vorpal sword in hand:
   Long time the manxome foe he sought—
So rested he by the Tumtum tree,
   And stood awhile in thought.

And as in uffish thought he stood,
   The Jabberwock, with eyes of flame,
Came whiffling through the tulgey wood,
   And burbled as it came!

One, two! One, two! And through and through
   The vorpal blade went snicker-snack!
He left it dead, and with its head
   He went galumphing back.

'And hast thou slain the Jabberwock?
   Come to my arms, my beamish boy!
O frabjous day! Callooh! Callay!'
   He chortled in his joy.

'Twas brillig, and the slithy toves
   Did gyre and gimble in the wabe;
All mimsy were the borogoves,
   And the mome raths outgrabe.

LEWIS CARROLL

THE HEFFALUMPS

They gorgon on the gridges,
And they bathe in gummy gools,
   They raddle round the rolders
   With their alabaster stools.
They inhabit carawodgities,
In groups of seven or eight,
   And in the sugger seasons,
   They attempt to hibernate.
They walk by alliwaddling,
And go for runny trots.
   They cultivate gardenias
   In alabaster pots.
They rallow with the Rurigines,
And wallow in the wough (wuff).
   And muddihydrenate themselves
   With slimy gooly stuff.
They eat the lumptious bumberworm
With honey-bottomed bees
   And drink the gooly waters
   Under harawurly trees.
They greet their friends by horrolling
And make a grooly din.
They scratch their shilly feet
   Against their rinkle-ringy skin.
They shelter under hoolah trees
From splurgipuddling rain
   And when it is uphottening
   They waddle out again.
Their bodies are of greyish hue
With undulating humps,
   They're really quite boristical
   The rhiny heffalumps!

ROSEMARY MARRIOTT

70

THE JUMBLIES

They went to sea in a Sieve, they did,
   In a Sieve they went to sea:
In spite of all their friends could say
On a winter's morn, on a stormy day,
   In a Sieve they went to sea!
And when the Sieve turned round and round,
And every one cried, "You'll all be drowned!"
They called aloud, "Our Sieve ain't big,
"But we don't care a button! we don't care a fig!
   "In a Sieve we'll go to sea!"
     Far and few, far and few,
       Are the lands where the Jumblies live;
       Their heads are green, and their hands are blue,
       And they went to sea in a Sieve.

They sailed away in a Sieve, they did,
   In a Sieve they sailed so fast,
With only a beautiful pea-green veil
Tied with a riband by way of a sail,
   To a small tobacco-pipe mast;
And every one said, who saw them go,
"O won't they be soon upset, you know!
"For the sky is dark, and the voyage is long,
"And happen what may, it's extremely wrong
   "In a Seive to sail so fast!"
     Far and few, far and few,
       Are the lands where the Jumblies live;
       Their heads are green, and their hands are blue,
       And they went to sea in a Sieve.

The water it soon came in, it did,
   The water it soon came in;
So to keep them dry, they wrapped their feet
In a pinky paper all folded neat,
   And they fastened it down with a pin.

And they passed the night in a crockery-jar,
And each of them said, "How wise we are!
"Though the sky be dark, and the voyage be long,
"Yet we never can think we were rash or wrong,
    "While round in our Sieve we spin!"
        Far and few, far and few,
            Are the lands where the Jumblies live;
            Their heads are green, and their hands are blue,
            And they went to sea in a Sieve.

And all night long they sailed away;
    And when the sun went down,
They whistled and warbled a moony song
To the echoing sound of a coppery gong,
    In the shade of the mountains brown.
"O Timballo! How happy we are,
"When we live in a Sieve and a crockery-jar.
"And all night long in the moonlight pale,
"We sail away with a pea-green sail,
    "In the shade of the mountains brown!"
        Far and few, far and few,
            Are the lands where the Jumblies live;
            Their heads are green, and their hands are blue,
            And they went to sea in a Sieve.

They sailed to the Western Sea, they did,
    To a land all covered with trees,
And they bought an Owl, and a useful Cart,
And a pound of Rice, and a Cranberry Tart,
    And a hive of silvery Bees.
And they bought a Pig, and some green Jackdaws,
And a lovely Monkey with lollipop paws,
And forty bottles of Ring-Bo-Ree,
    And no end of Stilton Cheese.
        Far and few, far and few,
            Are the lands where the jumblies live;

Their heads are green, and their hands are blue,
    And they went to sea in a Sieve.

And in twenty years they all came back,
  In twenty years or more,
And every one said, "How tall they've grown!
"For they've been to the Lakes, and the Terrible
      Zone,
    "And the hills of the Chankly Bore;"
And they drank their health, and gave them a feast
Of dumplings made of beautiful yeast;
And every one said, "If we only live,
"We too will go to sea in a Sieve, —
  "To the hills of the Chankly Bore!"
    Far and few, far and few,
      Are the lands where the Jumblies live;
    Their heads are green, and their hands are blue,
      And they went to sea in a Sieve.

EDWARD LEAR

Dance Drama

from CHORUS NO. 7 from "THE ROCK"

In the beginning GOD created the world. Waste and void.
Waste and void. And darkness was upon the face of
the deep.
And when there were men, in their various ways, they
struggled in torment towards GOD
Blindly and vainly, for man is a vain thing, and man with-
out GOD is a seed upon the wind: driven this way
and that, and finding no place of lodgement and
germination.
They followed the light and the shadow, and the light
led them forward to light and the shadow led them
to darkness.
Worshipping snakes or trees, worshipping devils rather
than nothing: crying for life beyond life, for ecstasy
not of the flesh.
Waste and void. Waste and void. And darkness on the
face of the deep.

And the Spirit moved upon the face of the water
And men who turned towards the light and were known
of the light
Invented the Higher Religions; and the Higher Religions
were good
And led men from light to light, to knowledge of Good
and Evil.
But their light was ever surrounded and shot with dark-
ness
As the air of temperate seas is pierced by the still dead
breath of the Arctic Current;

74

And they came to an end, a dead end stirred with a
        flicker of life,
And they came to the withered ancient look of a child
        that has died of starvation.
Prayer wheels, worship of the dead, denial of this world,
        affirmation of rites with forgotten meanings
In the restless wind-whipped sand, or the hills where the
        wind will not let the snow rest.
Waste and void. Waste and void. And darkness on the
        face of the deep.

  Then came, at a predetermined moment, a moment in
        time and of time,
A moment not out of time, but in time, in what we call
        history; transecting, bisecting the world of time, a
        moment in time but not like a moment of time,
A moment in time but time was made through that moment:
        for without the meaning there is no time, and
        that moment of time gave the meaning.
Then it seemed as if men must proceed from light to
        light, in the light of the Word,
Through the Passion and Sacrifice saved in spite of their
        negative being;
Bestial as always before, carnal, self-seeking as always
        before, selfish and purblind as ever before,
Yet always struggling, always reaffirming, always re-
        suming their march on the way that was lit by the
        light;
Often halting, loitering, straying, delaying, returning,
        yet following no other way.

  But it seems that something has happened that has
        never happened before: though we know not just
        when, or why, or how, or where.
Men have left GOD not for other gods, they say, but for
        no god; and this has never happened before
That men both deny gods and worship gods, professing

first Reason,
And then Money, and Power, and what they call Life, or
    Race, or Dialectic.
The Church disowned, the tower overthrown, the bells
    upturned, what have we to do
But stand with empty hands and palms turned upwards
In an age which advances progressively backwards?

T.S. ELIOT

LORD OF THE DANCE

I danced in the morning
    when the world was begun,
And I dance in the moon
    and the stars and the sun,
And I came down from heaven
    and I danced on the earth;
At Bethlehem
    I had my birth:

Dance, then, wherever you may be;
I am the Lord of the Dance, said he,
And I'll lead you all, wherever you
        may be,
And I'll lead you all in the dance,
        said he.

I danced for the scribe
    and the pharisee,
But they would not dance
    and they wouldn't follow me;
I danced for the fishermen,
    for James and John;
They came with me
    and the dance went on:

I danced on the Sabbath
   and I cured the lame:
The holy people
   said it was a shame.
They whipped and they stripped
   and they hung me high,
And they left me there
   on a cross to die:

I danced on a Friday
   when the sky turned black;
It's hard to dance
   with the devil on your back.
They buried my body
   and they thought I'd gone;
But I am the dance
   and I still go on:

They cut me down
   and I leap up high;
I am the life
   that'll never, never die;
I'll live in you
   if you'll live in me:
I am the Lord
   of the Dance, said he:

SYDNEY CARTER

77

EPITAPH

I think they will remember this as the age of lamentations,
The age of broken minds and broken souls,
The age of hurt creatures sobbing out their sorrow to the
     rythm of the blues—
The music of lost Africa's desolation become the music of
     the town.

The age of failure of splendid things,
The age of the deformity of splendid things,
The age of old young men and bitter children,
The age of treachery and of a great new faith.
The age of madness and machines,
Of broken bodies and fear twisted hearts,

The age of frenzied fumbling and possessive lusts—
And yet, deep down, an age unsatisfied by dirt and guns,
An age which though choked by the selfishness of the few
     who owned their bodies and their souls,
Still struggled blindly to the end,
And in their time reached out magnificently
Even for the very stars themselves.

H.D. CARBERRY

ON THE MOUNTAIN

The bones of the children cried out upon the mountain
Thin bones, bird bones, crying like birds
Up the glacier birdfooted tracks
Hens' feet crows' feet, old snow old world.

The blood of the children cried out upon pavements
The burnt flesh of children screamed in the cities.
All over the earth machines stopped
Animals were dumb men stood listening
And this terrible crying accused
  The men in gold braid who make wars
  The men in silk hats who make peace
  The men in leather jackets who make revolutions
  The men in frock coats who break revolutions.

Then from His throne spoke the Lord Jehovah
Saying: bring Me millstones
A mountain of hollow stones for the necks
Of those who offended these My children.
And He was angry, saying: let there be ocean
Unplumbed depths, bewildering fishes
For each transgressor one halter and one stone.
The angry waves roared Aaaahhhhh.

Still the bones of the children cried out
The blood cried from the cobblestones
The paper bones glittering on ice
The honey blood swarming with blue flies.
By the ocean-sea walked the Lord Jehovah
Thinking millenniums; about His feet
Cherubim played ducks and drakes
With the hollow stones. The sea said Hussshhhh.

He heard the feet of a million walking
Unhurried, firm, from valley and plain
Before them ran trembling those to be judged

Flapping and fumbling
Mouthing and mumbling
Stooping and stumbling

Over the icy stones
The men with gold eyes
The men with silk hands
The men with leather hearts
The men with no faces
To be judged: to be brought to judgement
Before the children's bones, on the holy mountain.

M.K.JOSEPH

THE IRISH BALLAD

About a maid I'll sing a song,
    Sing rickety-tickety-tin,
About a maid I'll sing a song
Who didn't have her fam'ly long,
Not only did she do them wrong,
    She did ev'ry one of them in, them in,
    She did ev'ry one of them in.

One morning in a fit of pique,
    Sing rickety-tickety-tin,
One morning in a fit of pique,
She drowned her father in the creek,
The water tasted bad for a week,
    And we had to make do with gin, with gin,
    We had to make do with gin.

Her mother she could never stand,
    Sing rickety-tickety-tin,
Her mother she could never stand,
And so a cyanide soup she planned.
The mother died with the spoon in her hand,
    And her face in a hideous grin, a grin,
    Her face in a hideous grin.

She set her sister's hair on fire,
    Sing rickety-tickety-tin,
She set her sister's hair on fire,
And as the smoke and flame rose high'r,
Danced around the funeral pyre,
    Playing a violin, —olin,
    Playing a violin.

She weighted her brother down with stones,
    Sing rickety-tickety-tin,
She weighted her brother down with stones,
And sent him off to Davy Jones.

All they ever found were some bones,
    And occasional pieces of skin, of skin,
    Occasional pieces of skin.

One day when she had nothing to do,
    Sing rickety-tickety-tin,
One day when she had nothing to do,
She cut her baby brother in two,
And served him up as an Irish stew,
    And invited the neighbours in, —bors in,
    Invited the neighbours in.

And when at last the police came by,
    Sing rickety-tickety-tin,
And when at last the police came by,
Her little pranks she did not deny.
To do so, she would have had to lie,
    And lying, she knew, was a sin, a sin,
    Lying, she knew, was a sin.

My tragic tale I won't prolong,
    Sing rickety-tickety-tin,
My tragic tale I won't prolong,
And if you do not enjoy my song,
You've yourselves to blame if it's too long,
    You should never have let me begin, begin
    You should never have let me begin.

TOM LEHRER

82

HER KIND

I have gone out, a possessed witch,
haunting the black air, braver at night;
dreaming evil, I have done my hitch
over the plain houses, light by light:
lonely thing, twelve-fingered, out of mind.
A woman like that is not a woman, quite.
I have been her kind.

I have found the warm caves in the woods,
filled them with skillets, carvings, shelves,
closets, silks, innumerable goods;
fixed the suppers for the worms and the elves:
whining, rearranging the disaligned.
A woman like that is misunderstood.
I have been her kind.

I have ridden in your cart, driver,
waved my nude arms at villages going by,
learning the last bright routes, survivor
where your flames still bite my thigh
and my ribs crack where your wheels wind.
A woman like that is not ashamed to die.
I have been her kind.

ANNE SEXTON

THE DANIEL JAZZ

Darius the Mede was a king and a wonder.
His eye was proud, and his voice was thunder.
He kept bad lions in a monstrous den.
He fed up the lions on Christian men.

Daniel was the chief hired man of the land.
He stirred up the jazz in the palace band.
He whitewashed the cellar. He shovelled in the coal.
And Daniel kept a-praying: 'Lord, save my soul.'
Daniel kept a-praying: 'Lord, save my soul.'
Daniel kept a-praying: 'Lord, save my soul.'

Daniel was the butler, swagger and swell.
He ran upstairs. He answered the bell.
And *he* would let in whoever came a-calling:
Saints so holy, scamps so appalling.
'Old man Ahab leaves his card.
Elisha and the bears are a-waiting in the yard.
Here comes Pharaoh and his snakes a-calling.
Here comes Cain and his wife a-calling.
Shadrach, Meshach and Abednego for tea.
Here comes Jonah and the whale,
And the *Sea*!

Here comes St Peter and his fishing-pole.
Here comes Judas and his silver a-calling.
Here comes old Beelzebub a-calling.'
And Daniel kept a-praying: 'Lord, save my soul.'
Daniel kept a-praying: 'Lord, save my soul.'
Daniel kept a-praying: 'Lord, save my soul.'

His sweetheart and his mother were Christian and meek.
They washed and ironed for Darius every week.
One Thursday he met them at the door:
Paid them as usual, but acted sore.
He said: 'Your Daniel is a dead little pigeon.

He's a good hard worker, but he talks religion.'
And he showed them Daniel in the lion's cage.
Daniel standing quietly, the lions in a rage.

His good old mother cried:—
'Lord, save him.'
And Daniel's tender sweetheart cried:—
'Lord, save him.'

And she was a golden lily in the dew.
And she was as sweet as an apple on the tree.
And she was as fine as a melon in the corn-field,
Gliding and lovely as a ship on the sea,
Gliding and lovely as a ship on the sea.
And she prayed to the Lord:—
'*Send* Gabriel. *Send* Gabriel.'

King Darius said to the lions:—
'Bite Daniel. Bite Daniel.
Bite him. Bite him. Bite him!'

Thus roared the lions:—
'We want Daniel, Daniel, Daniel.
We want Daniel, Daniel, Daniel.
Grrrrrrrrrrrrrrrrrrrrrrrrrrrrrrrr.
Grrrrrrrrrrrrrrrrrrrrrrrrrrrrrrrrrr.'
And Daniel did not frown,
Daniel did not cry.
He kept on looking at the sky.

And the Lord said to Gabriel:—
'Go chain the lions down,
Go chain the lions down,
Go chain the lions down,
Go chain the lions down.'
And *Gabriel* chained the lions,
And *Gabriel* chained the lions,
And *Gabriel* chained the lions,

And Daniel got out of the den,
And Daniel got out of the den,
And Daniel got out of the den.
And Darius said: 'You're a Christian child,'
Darius said: 'You're a Christian child,'
Darius said: 'You're a Christian child,'
And gave him his job again,
And gave him his job again,
And gave him his job again.

VACHEL LINDSAY

THE CONGO

1. *Their Basic Savagery*

Fat black bucks in a wine-barrel room,
Barrel-house kings, with feet unstable,
Sagged and reeled and pounded on the
     table,
Pounded on the table,
Beat an empty barrel with the handle of a
     broom,
Hard as they were able,
Boom, boom, BOOM,
With a silk umbrella and the handle of a
     broom,
Boomlay, boomlay, boomlay, BOOM.
THEN I had religion, THEN I had a vision.
I could not turn from their revel in derision.
THEN I SAW THE CONGO, CREEPING THROUGH
     THE BLACK,
CUTTING THROUGH THE FOREST WITH A
     GOLDEN TRACK.
Then along that riverbank
A thousand miles
Tattooed cannibals danced in files;
Then I heard the boom of the blood-lust
     song
And a thigh-bone beating on a tin-pan gong.
And "BLOOD" screamed the whistles and
     the fifes of the warriors,
"BLOOD" screamed the skull-faced lean
     witch-doctors,
"Whirl ye the deadly voo-doo rattle,
Harry the uplands,
Steal all the cattle,
Rattle-rattle, rattle-rattle,
Bing.

87

Boomlay, boomlay, boomlay, BOOM,"
A roaring, epic, rag-time tune
From the mouth of the Congo
To the Mountains of the Moon.
Death is an Elephant,
Torch-eyed and horrible,
Foam-flanked and terrible.
BOOM, steal the pygmies,
BOOM, kill the Arabs,
BOOM, kill the white men,
HOO, HOO, HOO.

Listen to the yell of Leopold's ghost
Burning in Hell for his hand-maimed host.
Hear how the demons chuckle and yell
Cutting his hands off, down in Hell.
Listen to the creepy proclamation,
Blown through the lairs of the forest-nation,
Blown past the white-ants' hill of clay,
Blown past the marsh where the butter-
      flies play:—
"Be careful what you do,
Or Mumbo-Jumbo, God of the Congo,
And all of the other
Gods of the Congo,
Mumbo-Jumbo will hoo-doo you,
Mumbo-Jumbo will hoo-doo you,
Mumbo-Jumbo will hoo-doo you."

THE PIED PIPER OF HAMELIN

Hamelin Town's in Brunswick,
  By famous Hanover city;
The River Weser, deep and wide,
Washes its walls on the southern side;
A pleasanter spot you never spied;
But, when begins my ditty,
Almost five hundred years ago,
To see the townsfolk suffer so
    From vermin, was a pity.

  Rats!
They fought the dogs, and killed the cats,
  And bit the babies in the cradles,
And ate the cheeses out of the vats,
  And licked the soup from the cooks' own ladles,
Split open the kegs of salted sprats,
Made nests inside men's Sunday hats,
And even spoiled the women's chats
  By drowning their speaking
  With shrieking and squeaking
In fifty different sharps and flats.

At last the people in a body
  To the Town Hall came flocking:
" 'Tis clear," cried they, "our mayor's a noddy;
  And as for our Corporation — shocking
To think we buy gowns lined with ermine
For dolts that can't or won't determine
What's best to rid us of our vermin!
You hope, because you're old and obese,
To find in the furry civic robe ease?
Rouse up, Sirs! Give your brains a racking
To find the remedy we're lacking,
Or, sure as fate, we'll send you packing!"
At this the Mayor and Corporation

Quaked with a mighty consternation.

An hour they sat in council;
　　At length the Mayor broke silence:
"For a guilder I'd my ermine gown sell,
　　I wish I were a mile hence!
It's easy to bid one rack one's brain —
I'm sure my poor head aches again,
I've scratched it so, and all in vain.
Oh for a trap, a trap, a trap!"
Just as he said this, what should hap
At the chamber door but a gentle tap?
"Bless us," cried the Mayor, "what's that?"
(With the Corporation as he sat,
Looking little though wondrous fat;
Nor brighter was his eye, nor moister
Than a too-long-opened oyster,
Save when at noon his paunch grew mutinous
For a plate of turtle green and glutinous.)
"Only a scraping of shoes on the mat?
Anything like the sound of a rat
Makes my heart go pit-a-pat!"

"Come in!" — the Mayor cried, looking bigger:
And in did come the strangest figure!
His queer long coat from heel to head
Was half of yellow and half of red;
And he himself was tall and thin,
With sharp blue eyes, each like a pin,
And light loose hair, yet swarthy skin,
No tuft on cheek nor beard on chin,
But lips where smiles went out and in —
There was no guessing his kith and kin!
And nobody could enough admire
The tall man and his quaint attire.
Quoth one: "It's as my great grandsire,
Starting up at the Trump of Doom's tone,

90

Had walked this way from his painted tomb—
    stone!"

He advanced to the council-table:
And, "Please your honours," said he, "I'm able,
By means of a secret charm, to draw
    All creatures living beneath the sun,
    That creep or swim or fly or run,
After me so as you never saw!
And I chiefly use my charm
On creatures that do people harm,
The mole and toad and newt and viper;
And people call me the Pied Piper."
(And here they noticed round his neck
    A scarf of red and yellow stripe,
To match his coat of the self-same check;
    And at the scarf's end hung a pipe;
And his fingers, they noticed, were ever straying
As if impatient to be playing
Upon this pipe, as low it dangled
Over his vesture so old-fangled.)
"Yet," said he, "poor piper as I am,
In Tartary I freed the Cham,
    Last June, from his huge swarm of gnats;
I eased in Asia the Nizam
    Of a monstrous brood of vampyre-bats:
And as for what your brain bewilders,
    If I can rid your town of rats
Will you give me a thousand guilders?"
"One? fifty thousand!" — was the exclamation
Of the astonished Mayor and Corporation.

Into the street The Piper stept,
    Smiling first a little smile,
As if he knew what magic slept
    In his quiet pipe the while;
Then, like a musical adept,

91

To blow the pipe his lips he wrinkled,
And green and blue his sharp eyes twinkled,
Like a candle-flame where salt is sprinkled;
And ere three shrill notes the pipe uttered,
You heard as if an army muttered;
And the muttering grew to a grumbling;
And the grumbling grew to a mighty rumbling;
And out of the houses the rats came tumbling,
Great rats, small rats, lean rats, brawny rats,
Brown rats, black rats, grey rats, tawny rats,
Grave old plodders, gay young friskers,
    Fathers, mothers, uncles, cousins,
Cocking tails and pricking whiskers,
    Families by tens and dozens,
Brothers, sisters, husbands, wives—
Followed the Piper for their lives.
From street to street he piped advancing,
And step by step they followed dancing,
Until they came to the river Weser
    Wherein all plunged and perished!
— Save one who, stout as Julius Cæsar,
Swam across and lived to carry
    (As he, the manuscript he cherished)
To Rat-land home his commentary:
Which was, "At the first shrill notes of the pipe,
I heard a sound as of scraping tripe,
And putting apples, wondrous ripe,
Into a cider-press's gripe:
And a moving away of pickle-tub-boards,
And a leaving ajar of conserve-cupboards,
And a drawing the corks of train-oil flasks,
And a breaking the hoops of butter casks:
And it seemed as if a voice
    (Sweeter far than by harp or by psaltery
Is breathed) called out, 'Oh rats, rejoice!
    The world is grown to one vast drysaltery!

So munch on, crunch on, take your nuncheon,
Breakfast, supper, dinner, luncheon!'
And just as a bulky sugar-puncheon,
All ready staved, like a great sun shone
Glorious scarce an inch before me,
Just as methought it said, 'Come, bore me!'
— I found the Weser rolling o'er me."

You should have heard the Hamelin people
Ringing the bells till they rocked the steeple.
"Go," cried the Mayor, "and get long poles!
Poke out the nests and block up the holes!
Consult with carpenters and builders,
And leave in our town not even a trace
Of the rats!" —when suddenly, up the face
Of the Piper perked in the market-place,
 With a, "First, if you please, my thousand
  guilders!"

A thousand guilders! The Mayor looked blue;
So did the Corporation too.
For council dinners made rare havoc
With Claret, Moselle, Vin-de-Grave, Hock;
And half the money would replenish
Their cellar's biggest butt with Rhenish.
To pay this sum to a wandering fellow
With a gipsy coat of red and yellow!
"Besides," quoth the Mayor, with a knowing wink,
"Our business was done at the river's brink;
We saw with our eyes the vermin sink,
And what's dead can't come to life, I think.
So, friend, we're not the folks to shrink
From the duty of giving you something for drink,
And a matter of money to put in your poke;
But as for the guilders, what we spoke
Of them, as you very well know, was in joke.
Besides, our losses have made us thrifty!"

A thousand guilders! Come, take fifty!"

The Piper's face fell, and he cried,
"No trifling! I can't wait, beside!
I've promised to visit by dinner time
Bagdat, and accept the prime
Of the Head-Cook's pottage, all he's rich in,
For having left, in the Caliph's kitchen,
Of a nest of scorpions no survivor:
With him I proved no bargain-driver,
With you, don't think I'll bate a stiver!
And folks who put me in a passion
May find me pipe after another fashion."

"How!" cried the Mayor, "d'ye think I'll brook
Being worse treated than a Cook?
Insulted by a lazy ribald
With idle pipe and vesture piebald?
You threaten us, fellow? Do your worst,
Blow your pipe there till you burst!"

Once more he stept into the street;
   And to his lips again
   Laid his long pipe of smooth straight cane;
And ere he blew three notes (such sweet
Soft notes as yet musician's cunning
   Never gave the enraptured air)
There was a rustling that seemed like a bustling
Of merry crowds justling at pitching and hustling,
Small feet were pattering, wooden shoes clattering,
Little hands clapping and little tongues chattering,
And, like fowls in a farm-yard when barley is
     scattering,
Out came the children running.
All the little boys and girls,
With rosy cheeks and flaxen curls,
And sparkling eyes and teeth like pearls,

Tripping and skipping, ran merrily after
The wonderful music with shouting and laughter.

The Mayor was dumb, and the Council stood
As if they were changed into blocks of wood,
Unable to move a step, or cry
To the children merrily skipping by —
Could only follow with the eye
That joyous crowd at the Piper's back.
But how the Mayor was on the rack,
And the wretched Council's bosoms beat,
As the Piper turned from the High Street
To where the Weser rolled its waters
Right in the way of their sons and daughters!
However he turned from South to West,
And to Koppelberg Hill his steps addressed,
And after him the children pressed;
Great was the joy in every breast.
"He never can cross that mighty top!
He's forced to let the piping drop,
And we shall see our children stop!"
When, lo, as they reached the mountain's side,
A wondrous portal opened wide,
As if a cavern was suddenly hollowed;
And the Piper advanced and the children followed,
And when all were in to the very last,
The door in the mountain-side shut fast.
Did I say all? No! One was lame,
    And could not dance the whole of the way;
And in after years, if you would blame
    His sadness, he was used to say, —
"It's dull in our town since my playmates left!
I can't forget that I'm bereft
Of all the pleasant sights they see,
Which the Piper also promised me.
For he led us, he said, to a joyous land,

Joining the town and just at hand,
Where waters gushed and fruit-trees grew,
And flowers put forth a fairer hue,
And everything was strange and new;
The sparrows were brighter than peacocks here,
And their dogs outran our fallow deer,
And honey-bees had lost their stings,
And horses were born with eagles' wings:
And just as I became assured
My lame foot would be speedily cured,
The music stopped and I stood still,
And found myself outside the hill,
Left alone against my will,
To go now limping as before,
And never hear of that country more!"

Alas, alas for Hamelin!
    There came into many a burgher's pate
    A text which says that Heaven's Gate
    Opes to the rich at as easy rate
As the needle's eye takes a camel in!
The Mayor sent East, West, North, and South,
To offer the Piper, by word of mouth,
    Wherever it was men's lot to find him,
Silver and gold to his heart's content,
If he'd only return the way he went,
    And bring the children behind him.
But when they saw 'twas a lost endeavour,
And Piper and dancers were gone for ever,
They made a decree that lawyers never
    Should think their records dated duly
If, after the day of the month and year,
These words did not as well appear,
"And so long after what happened here
    On the Twenty-second of July,
Thirteen hundred and seventy-six;"

And the better in memory to fix
The place of the children's last retreat,
They called it, the Pied Piper's Street—
Where any one playing on pipe or tabor
Was sure for the future to lose his labour.
Nor suffered they hostelry or tavern
    To shock with mirth a street so solemn:
But opposite the place of the cavern
    They wrote the story on a column,
And on the great church-window painted
The same to make the world acquainted
How their children were stolen away;
And there it stands to this very day.
And I must not omit to say
That in Transylvania there's a tribe
Of alien people that ascribe
The outlandish ways and dress
On which their neighbours lay such stress,
To their fathers and mothers having risen
Out of some subterraneous prison
Into which they were trepanned
Long time ago in a mighty band
Out of Hamelin town in Brunswick land,
But how or why, they don't understand.

So, Willy, let you and me be wipers
Of scores out with all men — especially pipers:
And, whether they pipe us free from rats or from
        mice,
If we've promised them aught, let us keep our
        promise!

ROBERT BROWNING

For the Young

JACK BE NIMBLE

Jack be nimble,
Jack be quick,
Jack jump over
The candlestick.

TRADITIONAL

THERE WAS A CROOKED MAN

There was a crooked man, and he went a crooked mile,
He found a crooked sixpence against a crooked stile;
He bought a crooked cat, which caught a crooked mouse,
And they all lived together in a little crooked house.

TRADITIONAL

THE SQUIRREL

Whisky, frisky,
  Hippity hop,
Up he goes
  To the tree top!

Whirly, twirly,
  Round and round,
Down he scampers
  To the ground.

Furly, curly,
   What a tail!
Tall as a feather,
   Broad as a sail!

Where's his supper?
   In the shell.
Snippity, crackity.
   Out it fell!

CHRISTINA ROSSETTI

THE SPIDER

The spider moves
on his web like
a tight-rope walker.

His web is like
lots of electric
lights at night.
The web glistens
in the light
like a mysterious trap.

DAVID BARNES

THE EAGLE

He clasps the crag with crooked hands;
Close to the sun in lonely lands,
Ringed with the azure world he stands.

The wrinkled sea beneath him crawls;
He watches from his mountain-walls,
And like a thunderbolt he falls.

LORD TENNYSON

99

FLYING CROOKED

The butterfly, a cabbage-white,
(His honest idiocy of flight)
Will never now, it is too late,
Master the art of flying straight,
Yet has — who knows so well as I? —
A just sense of how not to fly:
He lurches here and here by guess
And God and hope and hopelessness.
Even the aerobatic swift
Has not his flying-crooked gift.

ROBERT GRAVES

JACK FROST

    Look out! look out!
    Jack Frost is about!
He's after our fingers and toes;
    And, all through the night,
    The gay little sprite
Is working where nobody knows.

    He'll climb each tree,
    So nimble is he,
His silvery powder he'll shake;
    To windows he'll creep,
    And while we're asleep,
Such wonderful pictures he'll make.

    Across the grass,
    He'll merrily pass,
And change all its greenness to white;
    Then home he will go,
    And laugh, "Ho! ho! ho!
What fun I have had in the night!"

CECILY E. PIKE

STOCKING AND SHIRT

Stocking and shirt
   Can trip and prance,
Though nobody's in them
   To make them dance.
See how they waltz
   Or minuet,
Watch the petticoat
   Pirouette.
This is the dance
   Of stocking and shirt,
When the wind puts on
   The white lace skirt.
Old clothes and young clothes
   Dance together,
Twirling and whirling
   In the mad March weather.
'Come!' cries the wind,
   To stocking and shirt,
'Away!' cries the wind
   To blouse and skirt.
Then clothes and wind
   All pull together,
Tugging like mad
   In the mad March weather.
Across the garden
   They suddenly fly
And over the far hedge
   High, high, high!
'Stop!' cries the housewife,
   But all too late,
Her clothes have passed
   The furthest gate.

They are gone for ever
   In the bright blue sky,
And only the handkerchiefs
   Wave good-bye.

JAMES REEVES

DRY BONES

Dem bones dem bones dem dry bones,
Dem bones dem bones dem dry bones,
Dem bones dem bones dem dry bones,
Now hear the Word of the Lord.

    With your toe bone connected to your foot bone,
    Your foot bone connected to your heel bone,
    Your heel bone connected to your ankle bone,
    Your ankle bone connected to your leg bone,
    Your leg bone connected to your knee bone,
    Your knee bone connected to your thigh bone,
    Your thigh bone connected to your hip bone,
    Your hip bone connected to your back bone,
    Your back bone connected to your shoulder bone,
    Your shoulder bone connected to your neck bone,
    Your neck bone connected to your head bone,
    Now hear the Word of the Lord.

Dem bones dem bones gonna walk around,
Dem bones dem bones gonna walk around,
Dem bones dem bones gonna walk around,
Now hear the Word of the Lord.

Disconnect dem bones dem dry bones,
Disconnect dem bones dem dry bones,
Disconnect dem bones dem dry bones,
Now hear the Word of the Lord.

When your head bone's connected from your neck bone,
Your neck bone's connected from your shoulder bone,
Your shoulder bone's connected from your back bone,
Your back bone's connected from your hip bone,
Your hip bone's connected from your thigh bone,
Your thigh bone's connected from your knee bone,
Your knee bone's connected from your leg bone,
Your leg bone's connected from your ankle bone,
     Your ankle bone's connected from your heel bone,
     Your heel bone's connected from your foot bone,
     Your foot bone's connected from your toe bone,
     Now hear the Word of the Lord.

Dem bones dem bones dem dry bones,
Dem bones dem bones dem dry bones,
Dem bones dem bones dem dry bones,
Now hear the Word of the Lord.

TRADITIONAL

THE WITCH AND THE GOBLIN

The witch! The witch that lives in the wood,
She's not very pretty — she's not very good.
Her hair is brown and her eyes are black,
A firece old pussycat sits on her back
With a sharp thin tail sticking up like a spire,
While the mistress crouches over the fire,
Be the day cold or be the day hot,
Watching her strange little bubbling pot.

The Goblin — the dwarf that lives on the hill,
He lies in the heather so still, so still,
But on thick dark nights when there isn't a moon,
He puts on his cloak and his dancing shoon
And runs along as soft as a mouse
Till he comes to the door of the witch's house.
"Yo ho!" he cries, "It's junketing weather!"
And off they go on a spree together,
Off they go on the tail of the wind —
The great black pussycat sails behind.
Haven't you heard them banging about?
Haven't you heard them whistle and shout?
Oh — but I tell you — it's better to hide
When the witch and the goblin are out for a ride!

UNKNOWN

HIST WHIST

hist   whist
little ghostthings
tip-toe
twinkle-toe

104

little twitchy
witches and tingling
goblins
hob-a-nob hob-a-nob

little hoppy happy
toad in tweeds
little itchy mousies

with scuttling
eyes rustle and run and
hidehidehide
whist

whisk look out for the old woman
with the wart on her nose
what she'll do to yer
nobody knows

for she knows the devil ooch
the devil ouch
the devil
ach the great

green
dancing
devil
devil

devil
devil
      wheeEEE

E. E. CUMMINGS

THE DEATH DANCE OF THE WHIRLY GUMS

The Whirly Gums came out that night,
They came to dance in the green moon's light,
They run and jump and twist and turn,
Their big red feet tramp down the fern.
And then as the midnight hour draws near,
The female Whirly Gums appear,
With toothless grins and pointed chins
They strike up a tune on their Hammershins.
And harken now to their dreadful cry
The rattle of bones as they slowly die.
And now the music quick becomes
Their feet step to the beating drums.
With hair all wild, and beating hearts
They jerk and twist in fitful starts,
Their teeth fall out, their nails crack
As strength to dance the dancers lack.
Their tongues loll out, their temples throb
And one by one the dying mob
Sink down to death,
They danced to death.

ELIZABETH POWELL

THE ZOBO BIRD

Do you think we skip,
Do you think we hop,
Do you think we flip,
Do you think we flop,
Do you think we trip
This fearful measure
And hop and hip
For personal pleasure?

O no, o no,
We are full of woe
From top to toe:
It's the dread Zobo,
    The Zobo bird.

He brings us bane,
He brings us blight,
He brings us pain
By day and night:
And so we must
Though it take all day
Dance or bust
Till he flies away.

    Away, away!
    O don't delay.
      Go, Zobo, go,
        O Zobo bird!

FRANK A. COLLYMORE

SONG FROM CALLIRRHOË

I dance and dance! Another faun,
A black one, dances on the lawn.
He moves with me, and when I lift
My heels his feet directly shift:
I can't outdance him though I try;
He dances nimblier than I.
I toss my head, and so does he;
What tricks he dares to play with me!
I touch the ivy in my hair;
Ivy he has and finger there.
The spiteful thing to mock me so!
I will outdance him! Ho, ho, ho!

MICHAEL FIELD

107

ALL THE FUN

Here's all the Fun of the Fair! Come buy!
Chute, and swing, and a penny a shy!
    And the lamps will blaze at night—
The dangling lamps that drip and hiss
Where peppermint, candy and liquorice,
Bull's-eyes, hardbake, coconut-ice,
    Are a farthing, or less, a bite.

The gilded organs blare and groan,
Jack rides the skewbald, Ruth the roan,
    Finger and knee clutched tight.
Giddily galloping on they course . . .
But who is it sits the little blue horse?
What stranger straddles that dark little horse,
    Half hidden out of sight?

And when, all silent, dark, and still
Are tent and tree-top, meadow and hill,
    Merry-go-round and man,
When the autumn stars shine faint above,
And the barn-owl hoots from her secret grove,
And the shades of night begin to rove,
I wonder what he'll be dreaming of—
    The gypsy-boy in the Van.

WALTER DE LA MARE

THE END OF THE ROAD

In these boots and with this staff
Two hundred leaguers and a half
Walked I, went I, paced I, tripped I.
Marched I, held I, skelped I, slipped I,
Pushed I, panted, swung and dashed I;
Picked I, forded, swan and splashed I,
Strolled I, climbed I, crawled and scrambled,
Dropped and dipped I, ranged and rambled;
Plodded I, hobbled I, trudged and tramped I,
And in lonely spinnies camped I,
Lingered, loitered, limped and crept I,
Clambered, halted, stepped and leapt I,
Slowly sauntered, roundly strode I,
And . . .
Let me not conceal it . . . rode I.

(For who but critics could complain
Of 'riding' in a railway train?)

Across the valleys and the high land,
With all the world on either hand,
Drinking when I had a mind to,
Singing when I felt inclined to:
Nor ever turned my face to home
Till I had slaked my heart at Rome.

HILAIRE BELLOC

SPANISH WATERS

Spanish waters, Spanish waters, you are ringing in my
 ears,
Like a slow sweet piece of music from the grey forgotten
 years;
Telling tales, and beating tunes, and bringing weary
 thoughts to me
Of the sandy beach at Muertos, where I would that I
 could be.

There's a surf breaks on Los Muertos, and it never stops
 to roar,
And it's there we came to anchor, and it's there we
 went ashore,
Where the blue lagoon is silent amid snags of rotting
 trees,
Dropping like the clothes of corpses cast up by the seas.

We anchored at Los Muertos when the dipping sun was
 red,
We left her half-a-mile to sea, to west of Nigger Head;
And before the mist was on the Cay, before the day was
 done,
We were all ashore on Muertos with the gold that we
 had won.

We bore it through the marshes in a half-score battered
 chests,
Sinking, in the sucking quagmires to the sunburn on our
 breasts,
Heaving over tree-trunks, gasping, damning at the flies
 and heat,
Longing for a long drink, out of silver, in the ship's cool
 lazareet.

The moon came white and ghostly as we laid the treasure
 down,

There was gear there'd make a beggarman as rich as
          Lima Town,
Copper charms and silver trinkets from the chests of
          Spanish crews,
Gold doubloons and double moidores, louis d'ors and
          portagues,

Clumsy yellow-metal earrings from the Indians of Brazil,
Uncut emeralds out of Rio, bezoar stones from Guayaquil;
Silver, in the crude and fashioned, pots of old Arica
          bronze,
Jewels from the bones of Incas desecrated by the Dons.

We smoothed the place with mattocks, and we took and
          blazed the tree,
Which marks yon where the gear is hid that none will
          ever see,
And we laid aboard the ship again, and south away we
          steers,
Through the loud surf of Los Muertos which is beating
          in my ears.

I'm the last alive that knows it. All the rest have gone
          their ways
Killed, or died, or come to anchor in the old Mulatas
          Cays,
And I go singing, fiddling, old and starved and in despair,
And I know where all that gold is hid, if I were only
          there.

It's not the way to end it all. I'm old, and nearly
          blind,
And an old man's past's a strange thing, for it never
          leaves his mind.
And I see in dreams, awhiles, the beach, the sun's disc
          dipping red,
And the tall ship, under topsails, swaying in past Nigger
          Head.

111

I'd be glad to step ashore there. Glad to take a pick and
    go
To the lone blazed coco-palm tree in the place no others
    know,
And lift the gold and silver that has mouldered there
    for years
By the loud surf of Los Muertos which is beating in my
    ears.

JOHN MASEFIELD

For Advanced Study

ONE AFTERNOON

It was a most beautiful
afternoon.
The rich smell of the long green grass
was overpowering.
And we lay in the long green
grass.
And felt the soft caress of the blades.
It was so quiet
we could almost hear the billowing of the
clouds.
As we lay in the long green grass
hand in hand.
Then we kissed
quickly.
And for a moment we were able to leave
this world of hate and
sorrow.
Then we kissed again
and this time you kissed hard and greedily
in the beauty and
quiet
of the afternoon and the long green grass.
And a feeling of nausea
came over me—
because you had spoilt it all by being
greedy.

MARTIN PEPLER

113

AS A MAN VENTURING

As a man venturing over the saltings
On a misty day, feeling the damp
Clog at his collar and the marsh
Ride dull and heavy on his boots,
And all the sights of the day, familiar in the sun,
Transformed and hidden in the mystery
Of the still, salt mist,
Suddenly stumbles on a stone,
He pauses, alone, half chilled with terror,
At this violation of the immense
Unrealized stillness that enfolds him.
And then, right at his feet, rousing the dark,
The redshank, the warden of the marshes,
Rings out his warning through the mist,
Shrill as a sudden entry of the strings,
Above the hidden music of the sea.
The cries of gull and curlew
Shout in the silence; a sudden clamour
And beat of angry rhythm, as a host
Of frightened wings tatters the darkness;
A sudden thronging of all the wastes of grey
With shadowy forms; a half seen flash
Of black and white and orange . . .
And then the mists roll in again
And the sound merges and is lost
In the ceaseless mutter of the far-off sea.

B. CAVE-BROWNE-CAVE

THE LABYRINTH

Since I emerged that day from the labyrinth,
Dazed with the tall and echoing passages,
The swift recoils, so many I almost feared
I'd meet myself returning at some smooth corner,
Myself or my ghost, for all there was unreal
After the straw ceased rustling and the bull
Lay dead upon the straw and I remained,
Blood-splashed, if dead or alive I could not tell
In the twilight nothingness (I might have been
A spirit seeking his body through the roads
Of intricate Hades) — ever since I came out
To the world, the still fields swift with flowers, the trees
All bright with blossom, the little green hills, the sea,
The sky and all in movement under it,
Shepherds and flocks and birds and the young and old,
(I stared in wonder at the young and the old,
For in the maze time had not been with me;
I had strayed, it seemed, past sun and season and change,
Past rest and motion, for I could not tell
At last if I moved or stayed; the maze itself
Revolved around me on its hidden axis
And swept me smoothly to its enemy,
The lovely world) —since I came out that day,
There have been times when I have heard my footsteps
Still echoing in the maze, and all the roads
That run through the noisy world, deceiving streets
That meet and part and meet, and rooms that open
Into each other — and never a final room—
Stairways and corridors and antechambers
That vacantly wait for some great audience,
The smooth sea-tracks that open and close again,
Tracks undiscoverable, indecipherable,
Paths on the earth and tunnels underground,
And bird-tracks in the air — all seemed a part

Of the great labyrinth. And then I'd stumble
In sudden blindness, hasten, almost run,
As if the maze itself were after me
And soon must catch me up. But taking thought,
I'd tell myself, 'You need not hurry. This
Is the firm good earth. All roads lie free before you.'
But my bad spirit would sneer, 'No, do not hurry.
No need to hurry. Haste and delay are equal
In this one world, for there's no exit, none,
No place to come to, and you'll end where you are,
Deep in the centre of the endless maze.'

I could not live if this were not illusion.
It is a world, perhaps; but there's another.
For once in a dream or trance I saw the gods
Each sitting on the top of his mountain-isle,
While down below the little ships sailed by,
Toy multitudes swarmed in the harbours, shepherds drove
Their tiny flocks to the pastures, marriage feasts
Went on below, small birthdays and holidays,
Ploughing and harvesting and life and death,
And all permissible, and all acceptable,
Clear and secure as in a limpid dream.
But they, the gods, as large and bright as clouds,
Conversed across the sounds in tranquil voices
High in the sky above the untroubled sea;
And their eternal dialogue was peace
Where all these things were woven; and this our life
Was as a chord deep in that dialogue,
As easy utterance of harmonious words,
Spontaneous syllables bodying forth a world.

That was the real world; I have touched it once,
And now shall know it always. But the lie,
The maze, the wild-wood waste of falsehood, roads
That run and run and never reach an end,

Embowered in error — I'd be prisoned there
But that my soul has birdwings to fly free.

Oh these deceits are strong almost as life.
Last night I dreamt I was in the labyrinth,
And woke far on. I did not know the place.

EDWIN MUIR

IN BROKEN IMAGES

He is quick, thinking in clear images;
I am slow, thinking in broken images.

He becomes dull, trusting to his clear images;
I become sharp, mistrusting my broken images.

Trusting his images, he assumes their relevance;
Mistrusting my images, I question their relevance.

Assuming their relevance, he assumes the fact;
Questioning their relevance, I question the fact.

When the fact fails him, he questions his senses;
When the fact fails me, I approve my senses.

He continues quick and dull in his clear images;
I continue slow and sharp in my broken images.

He in a new confusion of his understanding;
I in a new understanding of my confusion.

ROBERT GRAVES

HIROSHIMA

Noon, and hazy heat;
A single silver sliver and a dull drone;
The gloved finger poised, pressed:
A second's silence, and
Oblivion.

ANON

WE SHALL OVERCOME

We shall overcome, we shall overcome,
    We shall overcome some day;
Oh, deep in my heart I do believe
    We shall overcome some day.

We shall walk in peace, we shall walk in peace,
    We shall walk in peace some day;
Oh, deep in my heart I do believe
    We shall walk in peace some day.

We shall all be free, we shall all be free,
    We shall all be free some day;
Oh, deep in my heart I do believe
    We shall all be free some day.

We shall learn to love, we shall learn to love,
    We shall learn to love some day;
Oh, deep in my heart I do believe
    We shall learn to love some day.

UNKNOWN

HEALING OF A LUNATIC BOY

Trees turned and talked to me,
Tigers sang,
Houses put on leaves,
Water rang.
Flew in, flew out
On my tongue's thread
A speech of birds
From my hurt head.

At my fine loin
Fire and cloud kissed,
Rummaged the green bone
Beneath my wrist.
I saw a sentence
Of fern and tare
Write with loud light
The mineral air.

On a stopped morning
The city spoke,
In my rich mouth
Oceans broke.
No more on the spun shore
I walked unfed.
I drank the sweet sea,
Stones were bread.

Then came the healer
Grave as grass,
His hair of water
And hands of glass.
I watched at his tongue
The white words eat,
In death, dismounted
At his stabbed feet.

Now river is river
And tree is tree,
My house stands still
As the northern sea.
On my hundred of parables
I heard him pray,
Seize my smashed world,
Wrap it away.

Now the pebble is sour,
The birds beat high,
The fern is silent,
The river dry.
A seething summer
Burned to bone
Feeds at my mouth
But finds a stone.

CHARLES CAUSLEY

PARLOUR-PIECE

With love so like fire they dared not
Let it out into strawy small talk;
With love so like a flood they dared not
Let out a trickle lest the whole crack,

These two sat speechlessly:
Pale cool tea in tea-cups chaperoned
Stillness, silence, the eyes
Where fire and flood strained.

TED HUGHES

THE LEAPING LAUGHERS

When will men again
Lift irresistible fists
Not bend from ends
But each man lift men
Nearer again.

Many men mean
Well: but tall walls
Impede, their hands bleed and
They fall, their seed the
Seed of the fallen.

See here the fallen
Stooping over stones, over their
Own bones: but all
Stooping doom beaten.

Whom the noonday washes
Whole, whom the heavens compel,
And to whom pass immaculate messages,
When will men again
Lift irresistible fists
Impede impediments
Leap mountains laugh at walls?

G. BARKER

NOTES

The following notes are suggestions that may be found useful. They are by no means comprehensive, nor are they intended to be strictly adhered to. We hope that they will stimulate thought on the most appropriate form of translation. Most poems have no notes, either because the contents are straightforward, or because their possibilities are so wide and numerous, that the teacher will be able to select whatever is most suitable for his group.

POEM BY T.S. ELIOT

We are most grateful to Faber and Faber Ltd. for allowing us to print a poem by T.S. Eliot. However, this permission was granted on the understanding that no public performances of dances based on T.S. Eliot's poem should be given. We would therefore ask our readers to see that this does not occur.

FANTASY

Dance evolving from exaggerated mime actions will best tell the story of most of these poems. Whole body involvement will be essential to achieve the varied characterizations. Children may like to add their own noises and props.

'Unwelcome' Mary Coleridge

The changes in a group caused by the passage of the woman and the man amongst them are the important elements here. The changes may be in the group's shape and intention or their actions and movement qualities.

THE SKY

'The Nature of Matter and Energy' Percy Bysshe Shelley

The harmonious movements within one's personal space might be explored, followed by relating these patterns to those of a partner, a small group or the whole class. The awareness of the "unimaginable shapes" within the pathways might be a further area of study.

'Fireworks' James Reeves

'Fourth of July Night' Carl Sandburg

Work on the movements mentioned making full use of the body can be explored by the class. This could lead to individual compositions or a massed display — possibly including appropriate vocal sounds or percussion.

122

WEATHER

'The Snowflake' Walter de la Mare
'London Snow' Robert Bridges
   The quality of a single snowflake and the massed impression of snow on trees, streets and buildings are described within these poems. Material for individual and group work on pattern and shape is readily found. Further possibilities are more dramatically based and include the effect of the snow on the movements and attitudes of humans.

WATER

   Contrasts in the motion and quality of water can form the starting point for varied activities. The more descriptive and scenic aspects of these poems will be built up with attention to effort. In some cases verses present a contrast to each other, in others the poem may be treated as a continuous whole.
'Port of Holy Peter' John Masefield
   Moments of mime or dance drama will probably be essential to this poem, possibly linked by a repetitive movement motif for the refrain. Small groups might like to work quite separately on different verses.
'The Cataract of Lodore' Robert Southey
   Almost any two lines from the descriptive section of this poem would serve as a good starting point for movement study. No mention need be made of water — in fact this is one poem that the teacher could use as a source of material, and never introduce in its entirety to a class.

THE COUNTRYSIDE

'Rain on Dry Ground' Christopher Fry
'The Burning of the Leaves' Laurence Binyon
   Each of these poems is concerned with a pattern of growth. This whole theme could be interpreted in dance, or certain specific ideas may be singled out for study, for example "the flagellant rain" from "Rain on Dry Ground".
'Humming Bird' D.H. Lawrence
'Bare Almond Trees' D.H. Lawrence
   The slow creation of a primeval jungle world of strangely shaped plants is in direct contrast to the sudden darting pathway of the humming bird. The stark linear shapes of the almond trees stand clearly against the soft vague background of grass. Both contrasts could be explored fully as movement opposites in the body.

MACHINES

'The Express' Stephen Spender
   The final result of working on this poem may well be that movement

qualities have been experienced rather than a 'dance' produced. First practical implications are those of speed increase and mechanical rhythm, but it is also possible to interpret the poem more widely in the context of bound flow becoming free flow.

'The American Railway' Traditional

The strong repetitive rhythm of this poem can be used to stimulate lively working actions or to accompany travelling patterns.

'Lines' Deborah Bestwick

The first verse suggests many possibilities for straight-forward movement study of visual patterns made by individuals and groups. The second and third contain dramatic ideas that could be developed from this exploration.

'The Secret of the Machines' Rudyard Kipling

This poem could stimulate work on machinery in general or on a particular type of machine mentioned. Alternatively the idea could be treated more philosophically, considering the all powerful machine as both the child of man and the destroyer of man.

PEOPLE

'People' D.H. Lawrence

Work on awareness of one's own personal space and its relation to that of others helps to express this idea vividly in movement.

'maggie and milly and molly and may' E.E. Cummings

At a simple level use of this poem might well lead to the production of short dances in groups of four. The poem could however be developed more symbolically by an experienced group giving particular consideration to the last verse.

'The Feel of Hands' Thom Gunn

Awareness of how hands move and of their relationship with each other as well as to other parts of the body, are the primary concerns here. Sensitive group awareness involving touch could arise, and older classes may like to suggest an interpretation of the last verse.

'The Builders' Laurence Binyon

This poem might be used as a stimulus in the exploration of degrees of tension in the body, or as part of a wider dramatic theme.

'Prayer Before Birth' Louis MacNeice

The ideas in this poem are dramatic in nature, the happenings described are concerned with relationships between the world and the subject. The exact effort content relevant to each situation needs to be carefully planned and considered in relation to the group organization. The expression may be so specific that only a few confrontations can be developed.

124

HAPPENINGS

'Earthquake' James Kirkup

The central idea of imbalance where there has been balance, of bizarre movement where there has been stillness can be stressed and explored in a variety of ways. Alternatively the poem might lead to a drama, bringing in more disastrous effects of an earthquake and the reactions of people to the uncanny and shattering situation.

'Peace' D.H. Lawrence

The idea of a volcano, its eruption and the movement of the lava could be translated simply into movement. A more symbolic approach would be to explore peace in its contrast to chaos and destruction.

'Everyone Sang' Siegfried Sassoon

Here is the contrast to the last poem, complete freedom to enjoy space in free flow. After individual discovery group work might take the form of spreading into space, reforming only to disperse again.

'Bat' D.H. Lawrence

The two motion factors found in this poem are those of space and time. The eerie atmosphere may be obtained by stressing unusual air and floor patterns and by mastering rapid speed changes with very light tension. The human reaction to bats might suggest a different starting point.

NONSENSE

All these poems may be used as an aural accompaniment to the movement.

'They told me you had been to her' Lewis Carroll

This can make a situation comedy with the characters performing entries and actions as described in quick succession.

'Jabberwocky' Lewis Carroll
'The Heffalumps' Rosemary Marriott

The poems depend for their impact on the unusual visual images produced by the words. To translate them successfully into dance, time should be spent obtaining the most apt movement qualities for these unusual impressions. The dancers might subsequently enjoy inventing their own weird beings and creatures.

'The Jumblies' Edward Lear

With younger dancers the story will probably predominate, leading to dance drama. With an older group it will be possible to select and develop separate ideas in more symbolic form. Rhythms or repetitive parts could be developed in imaginative movement motifs which themselves could be varied each time they occurred, for example in the Jumblies' refrain.

125

DANCE DRAMA

'Lord of the Dance' Sydney Carter

Because of the enormity of the subject matter a full dramatic rendering of this poem would be a major undertaking. Repetitive gestures and simple representative actions could be woven into a group dance perhaps based on group shapes such as lines, circles or blocks. The dancers could move directly to the sound of the spoken poem or preferably to the song with its musical accompaniment. (Tune: Shaker. "100 Hymns for Today" published by the Proprietors of "Hymns Ancient and Modern".)

'Epitaph' H.D. Carberry

The idea of change in body shape as a movement theme might appropriately mirror the journey of the few through brokenness, failure and madness to a final solution. Grotesque and harmonious movement patterns would be contrasted here.

'On the Mountain' M.K. Joseph

The theme of the poem is the exploitation of the innocent. Groups of dancers could represent the oppressed and their oppressors and further ideas could include judgement on the 'faceless' by the 'million'.

'Irish Ballad' Tom Lehrer

This is an obvious poem for exaggerated dance-mime. Comic chorus movements could be invented and the whole performed to the record (Decca LK 4375 mono).

'Her Kind' Anne Sexton

This could form the basis of quite an involved and detailed dance drama, with the witch's activities, the villagers, a witch-hunt, mocking and burning all playing their parts.

'The Daniel Jazz' Vachel Lindsay
'The Congo' Vachel Lindsay

Both of these poems need to be spoken by a well-rehearsed, enthusiastic choral group while the movement takes place, as both depend on the sound of the Jazz idiom for their full impact. (This could be tape-recorded for practising purposes.) Just as different vocal qualities will be used and the speakers may be solo, or in small or large groups to give aural interest, corresponding movement ideas and groupings will probably be appropriate. It may be necessary for the development of the action to stop the chorus on occasion to enable a 'scene' to become more detailed. If so, this should be done with sensitivity to the aural development. One might also consider the dancers' joining in with certain lines or making other contributory sounds. Clapping and drum-beats might also stress the Jazz beat.

FOR THE YOUNG

Most of the shorter poems vividly describe the action of their subjects. These ideas will enable children to explore how their bodies move, for example: up and down, forwards, backwards and sideways,

126

twisting and turning and all the ways of travelling. Notes follow on the less straight-forward poems.

'The Squirrel' Christina Rosetti
'The Spider' David Barnes
'The Eagle' A. Tennyson
'Flying Crooked' Robert Graves

It is important to realise with these poems that to copy the appearance of any creature has little value. More may be gained by studying the significant characteristics of the movements described. This might be the powerful tension of the eagle or the erratic pathway of the butterfly.

'The Witch and the Goblin' Unknown

The whole group will enjoy trying all sorts of witch-like activities and showing the goblin's actions. Finally pairing a witch and a goblin will give opportunity for creating short dances, possibly while using the poem as a spoken accompaniment.

'hist whist' E.E. Cummings

A group may find it great fun to play and experiment with the lively movement implications in this poem. Vocal sounds made by the children, percussion noises and even props might spring from these ideas.

FOR ADVANCED STUDY

These poems are primarily intended for use at student and adult level and therefore we have presumed that much of the interpretation will be made by the dancers. We hope that they will stimulate discussion and give opportunity for considerable thought in movement terms and choreographic range. The ideas noted below may serve as starting points for consideration of some of the poems.

'Parlour Piece' Ted Hughes

The translation into movement of being unable to speak into being unable to touch, could be the dancer's solution to this pair relationship.

'As a Man Venturing' B. Cave-Browne-Cave

The physical reaction of the subject to his surroundings makes the movement basis for this poem. To illustrate the progressions of thought and feeling, use of gesture combined with an appropriate floor pattern would demand careful selection of effort attitudes and drives.

'In Broken Images' Robert Graves

Work in pairs or in two contrasting groups is suggested. Whatever movements are chosen to represent the two ways of thinking, the verses could give opportunity for interesting timing of the interplay between two sides — unison, 'question and answer', interlocking, opposing speeds etc. The verses could be methodically worked through or the general nature of each character exploited.

'Healing of a Lunatic Boy' Charles Causley

The gay off balance movements of the unknowing deranged boy

could be contrasted with the disillusioned, formal movements of the boy when he is cured. A middle section in groups or pairs, possibly incorporating mirroring or 'question and answer', would serve to balance the composition.

FURTHER READING

Dance

Preston-Dunlop, V. *A Handbook for Modern Educational Dance,* (Macdonald and Evans).

Russell, Joan *Creative Dance in the Primary School* (Macdonald and Evans).

Russell, Joan *Creative Dance in the Secondary School* (Macdonald and Evans).

Carroll, J. and Lofthouse, P. *Creative Dance for Boys* (Macdonald and Evans).

Bruce, V. and Tooke, J. *Lord of the Dance* (Pergamon).

Drama

Goodridge, Janet *Drama* (Heinemann Educational)

Wiles, John and Garrard, Alan *Leap to Life* (Chatto and Windus).

Hodgson J. and Richards, Ernest *Improvisation - Discovery and Creativity in Drama* (Methuen & Co., University Paperbacks).

Way, Brian *Development through Drama* (Longman, Education Today Series).

Poetry

Blackburn, Thomas (Editor) *Presenting Poetry* (Methuen).

Reeves, James *Teaching Poetry* (Heinemann).

Morris, Helen *Where's that Poem?* (Basil Blackwell).